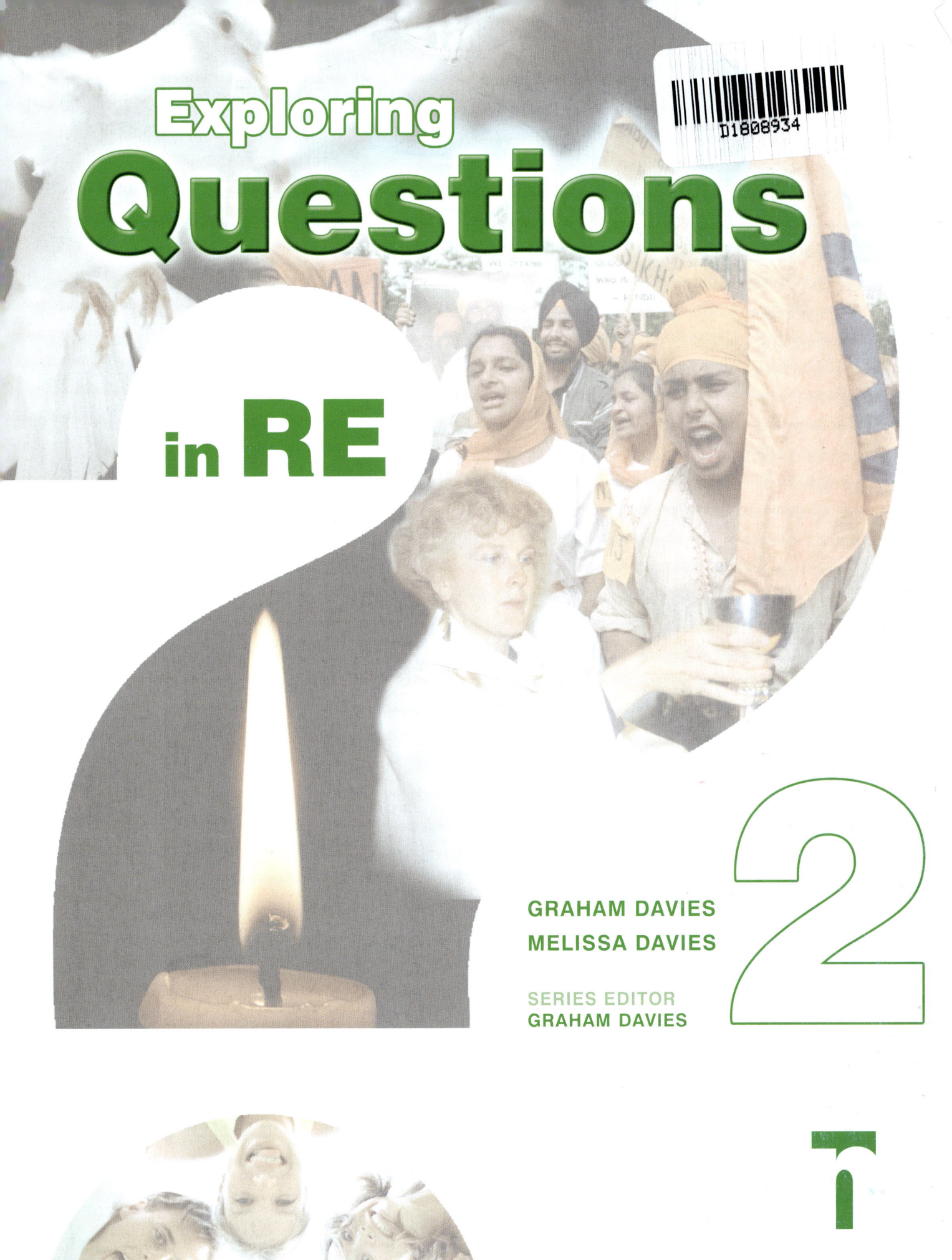

Exploring
Questions
in RE

GRAHAM DAVIES

MELISSA DAVIES

SERIES EDITOR
GRAHAM DAVIES

2

Published in 2005 by:
Nelson Thornes Ltd
Delta Place
27 Bath Road
CHELTENHAM
GL53 7TH
United Kingdom

05 06 07 08 09 / 10 9 8 7 6 5 4 3 2 1

A catalogue record for this book is available from the British Library

ISBN 0 7487 9363 1
Illustrations by Rupert Besley, Angela Lumley and Richard Morris
Picture research by Sue Sharp and Alison Prior
Edited by Melanie Gray
Page make-up by DP Press Ltd

Printed in Croatia by Zrinski

Acknowledgements
Action Plus Sports Images: 25, 40 (Tanni Grey Thompson); Akg Images: 10, 25 (centre), 33, 39 (centre right); Alamy/ Eddie Gerald: 11 (bottom); Alamy/ Photofrenetic: 7 (right); Alamy/ Photofusion: 9 (top), 46 (left); Alamy/ Photolibrary Wales: 46 (bottom right); Alamy/ World Religions: 55 (top); Andes Press Agency: 22 (top left), 54; Art Directors & Trip: 14 (bottom), 15 (bottom), 22 (bottom), 23 (bottom),49; Asian Christian Art Association: 35; Associated Press: 74; Bridgeman Art Library/LouvreParis: 93; Cafod: 84 (Cafod logo); Charlton News: 94; Christian Aid: 37(right), 84 (Christian Aid logo); Circa Photo Library/ Barrie Searle: 57 (F); Circa Photo Library/ John Smith: 22 (top right); Circa Photo Library/ William Holtby: 57 (H);Corbis: 8 (bottom right), 41 (middle right); Corbis/Al Arabiya: 26 (centre right); Corbis/Alexandra Winkler: 52 (left); Corbis/ Alison Wright: 20, 57 (top); Corbis/ Antoine Serra/ In Visu: 18; Corbis/Atef Hassan: 58 (top); Corbis/Bernard Bisson/Sygma: 30 (right), 38 (centre right); Corbis/ Bettman: 16 (both), 25 (Martin Luther King), 27 (top right), 70 (top right); Corbis/Brooks Craft: 25 (bottom); Corbis/ Chip East: 42 (top left); Corbis/Danilo Krstanovic/Reuters: 64 (top); Corbis/Earl & Nazima Kowall: 23 (top right); 47; Corbis/Fabio Polenghi: 36 (right); Corbis/GeraySweeney: 63 (top); Corbis/Howard Davies: 88 (bottom right); Corbis/ Hulton Deutsch: 43 (right); Corbis/ Jean-Paul Pelisser/ Reuters: 42 (right); Corbis/Jonathan Blair: 48; Corbis/Kim Kyung-Hoon: 30 (left); Corbis/Leif Skoogfors: (top), 37, 39 (top); Corbis/Lindsay Hebbard: 57 (centre right); Corbis/Marvel: 58 (bottom); Corbis/Maurice McDonald, Pool, Reuters: 70 (bottom); Corbis/Neal Preston: 95; Corbis/Nik Wheeler: 87; Corbis (NT): 36 (left), 56 (all), 90 (bottom right); Corbis/Olivier Coret/In Visu: 70 (centre right); Corbis/Owen Franken: 50 (bottom left); Corbis/Peter Turnely: 51; Corbis/ Reuters: 14 (top), 62 (left), 62 (centre), 88 (centre); Corbis/Reza;Webistan: 86; Corbis/Roger Ressmeyer: 32 (top); Corbis/Schultz Rene/Sygma: 64 (bottom); Corbis V94 (NT): 26 (bottom), 27 (bottom); Corel 62 (NT): 90 (D); Corel 353 (NT): 67 (top); 67 (top right); Corel 414 (NT): 58 (top); 76; Corel 654 (NT): 25 (Mother Teresa); 53 (Mother Teresa); Corel 678 (NT): 90 (E); Corel 793 (NT): 8 (top left); Corel 799 (NT): 25 (Nelson Mandela), 25 (Desmond Tutu); Digital Stock 4 (NT): 43 (bottom); 70 (left); Digital Stock 11 (NT): 88 (C); Dinodia: 19, 25 (Mahatma Gandhi); Empics/David Jones/PA: 67 (bottom); Empics/EPA: 62 (right), 68 (left & right), 80; Getty/AFP: 40 (top) , 76; Getty Images/David Rogers: 40 (top); Getty Images/David Roth: 32 (bottom); Illustrated London News V2 (NT): 75, 88 (A); Image 100 22 (NT): 52 (right); Graham Davies: 11, 23 (left); Ingram ILG (NT): 90 (B); Island Records: 45 (all); Israel Images/ Israel Talby: 32 (middle left), 41 (middle left); John Birdsall Social Issues Photo Library: 15 (top), 49 (top), 50 (left), 64 (right); Judith Wolfe, Dunedin, New Zealand www.arts.org.nz: 55 (bottom); Khalsa Aid: 65, 84 (Khalsa Aid sign); Kobal: 58 (centre); Martin Melaugh: 66; Muslim Aid: 84 (Muslim Aid logo); Offside Sports Photography: 40 (bottom left); PA Photos: 41 (top left); PA Photos/ Barry Batchelor: 41 (bottom right); PA Photos/ EPA: 44 (right); Photodisc 32 (NT): 39 (bottom); Photodisc 40 (NT): 52 (right); Photodisc 59B (NT): 59; Photodisc 5B (NT): 90 (A); Photodisc 66 (NT): 90 (C); Photofusion: 8 (bottom left), 50 (right); Photolibrary Wales/ Steve Benbow: 46 (top right), 57 (I); Popperfoto/Reuters: 57 (centre left); Rex Features Ltd: 7 (middle), 8 (top right), 9 (bottom), 25 (Christopher Reeve), 25 (Tupac Shakur), 40 (middle bottom), 41 (top right), 44 (left); Smile International: 53 (Smile logo); Tearfund: 81 (Tearfund logo); Tzedakah Project: 85; Tzedek: 84 (Tzedek logo); William Black, English, 1757-1827/The Temptation and Fall of Eve (Milton's "Paradise Lost")/1808. Pen and watercolour on Paper. Catalogue Raisonne: Butlin 536 (9), 49.7 x 38.7cm (19 9/16 x 15 _ in.) Museum of Fine Arts, Boston. Gift by subscription, 90.99. Copyright Museum of Fine Arts, Boston/Bridgeman Art Library): 29; VinMag Archive: 7 (left)

Contents

Introduction

We want you to be an excellent learner

In this book you will explore lots of questions about life and religion. This will involve finding out about beliefs and practices, ceremonies and rituals, as well as considering what members of faith communities think about those questions.

The questions aim to get you thinking about your own experiences of life, and help you to examine your feelings, values and beliefs. You will be encouraged to respond in your own words to pictures, questions and activities, sharing your views with others in your class. You will be able to listen to the opinions of others and to move forward in developing your own views and opinions.

We want you to be an excellent thinker

To be an excellent thinker, you need to:

- have a critical attitude to all the information you read. Never take anything for granted – question it
- keep an open mind – don't close down the possibilities too early
- ask lots of 'why' questions – try to work out the reasons for an action or viewpoint
- think about your thinking – give yourself some time to reflect on what you have read or discussed
- talk about your thinking – put your views into words. Listen carefully to the opinions of others and consider whether you need to adapt your view as a result
- look for connections between what you are learning now and what you have already learned. Try to see links with other religions or viewpoints.

We want you to develop these skills

- **Analysing what you are learning**: this might involve seeing patterns, organising different parts, making connections, making comparisons, explaining and interpreting.
- **Applying knowledge and understanding**: you can do this in a number of ways. For example, you might demonstrate, illustrate, modify and classify.
- **Empathy**: this involves being sensitive to the feelings and beliefs of others in the group. Put yourself in other people's shoes and see the world from their point of view.

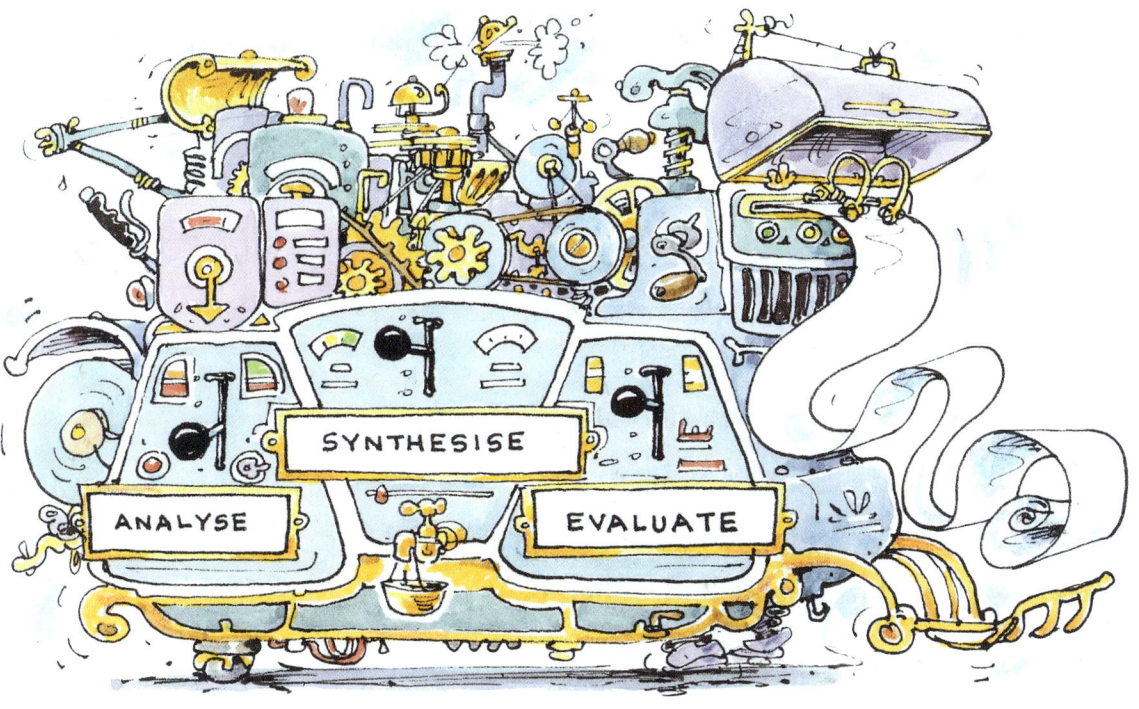

We want you to develop these skills too...

- **Enquiry**: you will need to research, investigate, observe and gather information from a number of sources, including books, sacred texts, CD-ROMs and websites.
- **Evaluation**: when you evaluate you make a judgement about how valuable, useful, accurate or meaningful something is. You might be putting something to the test, comparing ideas and making a decision about it.
- **Listening**: be an active listener. Focus on the person who is speaking and make some response either in your own mind or out loud to what is being said.
- **Making decisions**: to make meaningful decisions demands rigorous information gathering, careful consideration of the options, weighing up the advantages and disadvantages, deciding on the action and evaluating the outcomes.

- **Problem-solving**: you need to be able to tackle issues and problems, examine the evidence, look at the different possibilities, test solutions and come to conclusions.
- **Reasoning**: this is about giving reasons for opinions and actions, and making judgements and decisions informed by reasons or evidence.
- **Reflection**: this is an opportunity to consider what you have learned, examine your inner feelings, and consider some of the deeper questions of life. Other skills of being still and meditating are part of this.
- **Skills of synthesis**: this means bringing together and relating knowledge and understanding from different areas of study, drawing conclusions and building on what you know to think of new ideas.

This book will give you lots of opportunities to use and develop these skills as you read, discuss and engage in the variety of activities.

We wish you 'good thinking'!

This is about ...

- Understanding what a stereotype is
- Exploring different ways in which people stereotype others
- Knowing what prejudice is, and how it can lead to discrimination
- Investigating and reflecting on ways in which people have been discriminated against because of their religious beliefs
- Exploring and evaluating different religious teachings on equality
- Expressing your own views on stereotyping, prejudice and discrimination

Key questions

- What is stereotyping?
- Why are people stereotyped?
- What happens when people are **prejudiced**?
- Why is **discrimination** wrong?
- How have people challenged **inequality**?
- What do religions teach about equality?

Stereotyping is putting someone into a very simple category rather than looking at them as a person. For example, it's a **stereotype** to say that all professors are absent minded, or that all scientists are geeks. So, a stereotype is when we have a simplified idea of what someone is like based on characteristics we assume they share with others like them.

KEY WORDS

- Discrimination
- Inequality
- Prejudice
- Stereotype

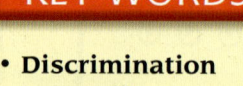

A

Bank manager   Sports store manager   Doctor

Nurse   Teacher   Social worker

OVER TO YOU

1 If you had to describe the type of people who have the jobs shown in picture **A**, what would you say they were like? Would they be men or women? What ages would they be? What colour skin do people who hold these jobs have?

2 Work with a partner. Produce a mind map starting with the word stereotype.

Help!

Mind map
A mind map starts with a main idea or topic at the centre of a page with branches to sub topics which branch out further again. Use drawings and colours as well as writing the connections along the branches.

Some stereotypes could be thought of as funny ideas that we have of people, like all grandmothers knit socks, or all farmers wear wellies. But some stereotypes are worrying because they show certain groups of people in a negative way. The problem with stereotyping is that the images given about a group are never true for everyone in it. For example, some older people might say all teenagers are vandals: is this true?

Fantastic Facts

Experts say we decide what we think about people in the first 7 to 17 seconds of meeting them – and it takes three times as long for us to change our mind from this first impression!

We usually make decisions about what someone is like based on first impressions of things like their clothes, hairstyle, age, colour, size, etc. However, our first impressions are often built on stereotypes. Stereotyping goes on all the time – in advertising, on television, in the workplace. We can even learn our stereotypes from friends and family without realising it.

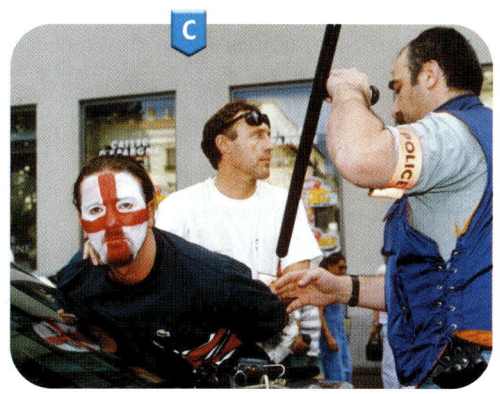

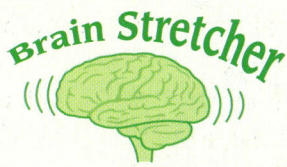

Brain Stretcher

We tend to think of stereotypes as being negative. Can you think of any positive stereotypes? Why do you think there are so many more negative stereotypes than positive ones?

OVER TO YOU

3 Look back at task 1. What descriptions did you come up with? Did you say whether each one would be a man or a woman? What ages did you give? What colour skin do people who hold these jobs have? Why did you make these decisions? Discuss the following questions with a partner.

a Do you think you were stereotyping?

b Where do you think your stereotypes come from?

4 Some stereotypes are well known and some are less obvious. How good are you at recognising stereotypes? Look at photos **B–D** and write down what stereotypes are being shown.

5 In small groups, sketch out short scenes that tell a story about stereotyping and what happens as a result. Once you have decided on your story, work out a series of freeze frames that you could perform.

Help!

Freeze frame

This involves setting up a scene as if it were a video freeze frame or a still from a movie. You need to choose a scene from the story and freeze it. You need to be able to describe how each character in the freeze frame is thinking and feeling at that precise moment.

What do we mean by prejudice and discrimination?

This is about ...

- **Understanding how stereotyping can lead to prejudice**
- **Making links between people's ideas and actions**
- **Identifying different forms of discrimination**
- **Thinking about your own behaviour towards other people**

Key questions

- **What does prejudice mean?**
- **Where do prejudices come from?**
- **What is discrimination?**
- **How are people discriminated against?**
- **How should I treat other people?**

KEY WORDS

- Discrimination
- Guru
- Kippah
- Prejudice
- Stereotype
- Turban

People develop **stereotypes** because of ignorance – making a decision about a person or a group of people before we know all the facts about them. In other words, we pre-judge them. People are usually prejudiced against others if they are different from themselves. This is because sometimes we can be afraid of the things we do not understand or are ignorant about.

When we allow our stereotypes to form our opinions about people, we develop prejudices. This is when we come to believe that our stereotypes about groups of people are real. As a result, we may not try to discover what some people are really like because we have already put them in a category. Prejudices can be positive things – like people from the USA are all friendly, for example – but they can also be negative.

How can prejudice lead to discrimination? When we take action as a result of our prejudices, this is known as discrimination. People can be discriminated against in many different ways.

OVER TO YOU

1 In pairs, look at photos **A–D** and see if you can work out the ways in which people are being discriminated against. Are there some pictures that do not show discrimination at all? Make your decisions with a partner, and then write them down.

A

B

C

D

NORTH CAROLINA LAW
White Patrons Please Seat From Front
Colored Patrons Please Seat From Rear
NO SMOKING

Sometimes, however, we can cause acts of discrimination to happen without meaning to. For instance, many Sikhs wear a turban as a requirement set down by the **Gurus** (Sikh leaders).

Jaswant, a young Sikh who has just started wearing his **turban**, explains why this is important to him.

> *I would not feel fully like a Sikh if I didn't wear my turban. It's like when my non-Sikh friends in school wear their favourite football team's shirt when they go to a match. It makes them feel like a true supporter of their team and everyone knows who they follow. My turban shows people who I am and what I believe in, and that I follow the word of God.*

Jaswant

It has not always been as easy as it should be for Sikhs to wear turbans in the UK. For example, it used to be hard for a Sikh to join the police force because police regulations said they had to wear a police helmet, which is obviously impossible to do while still wearing a turban! It was the same in other jobs where a certain type of headgear had to be worn.

Then, in the 1970s, the government passed a law requiring everyone who rides a motorbike to wear a helmet. Hundreds of Sikh motorcyclists protested against this because it meant taking off their turbans. Even though the law was not trying to discriminate against Sikhs, it treated them in a way that was against their religion. Eventually, the law was changed so that Sikhs did not have to wear a helmet.

E

In the 1970s, many Sikhs protested against a law that motorcyclists must wear helmets

OVER TO YOU

2 Do you think it is fair that Sikhs are treated differently from others because they wear a certain type of clothing, or do you think they should be made to follow the same law as non-Sikhs? Discuss this in pairs.

Faith • Faith • Faith • CONNECTIONS

Can you think of any other religions where wearing certain clothing is part of the faith, and where this could cause possible discrimination to happen?

3 Look at photo **E**. How do you think the person in the photo is feeling? Write down his diary entry for the day the photo was taken.

3 In March 2004, a law was passed in France that bans religious symbols and dress in the classroom. Schoolchildren are banned from wearing the Christian cross, Jewish **Kippah**, Islamic headscarf and Sikh turban. What are your feelings about this? What would you do if this ban affected you?

Why did the Holocaust happen?

This is about ...

- **Understanding what can happen when people act on their prejudices**
- **Responding to examples of religious discrimination**
- **Expressing your own views about the consequences of prejudice**
- **Remembering what prejudice and discrimination can do**

Key questions

- **How does religious prejudice show itself?**
- **What are the consequences of religious persecution?**
- **How can I stop religious persecution today?**

KEY WORDS

- **Concentration camp**
- **Discrimination**
- **Holocaust**
- **Nazi Party**
- **Persecution**
- **Prejudice**
- **Yad Vashem**

In the 1930s, a man named Adolf Hitler and his **Nazi Party** came to power in Germany. The Nazis believed the Germans were a special people and deserved more land to live in. This led to the Second World War when Germany invaded other countries.

The Nazis were extremely prejudiced against some groups of people, such as Jews, gypsies and homosexuals. They spread the prejudiced belief that these groups of people were dirty, caused problems for Germans and were inferior in every way to the German people. There were many Jews in Germany, and even more living in the countries of Eastern Europe that Hitler invaded.

Jewish people were **discriminated** against in many terrible ways under the Nazis:

- Families were moved out of their homes, businesses and jobs to live in the ghettos. Conditions were very bad; often families lived in one room and shared spaces with others, or some people had to live in makeshift shelters outside. There was very little food, and no proper sanitation so disease was common.

- Religious buildings and books were destroyed so that made it difficult to worship properly.

- Jews were made to wear markings of their religion in public. Normally people are proud to wear clothing and symbols that express something about their beliefs. However, Jews were made to do this so that people could mock and abuse them, for example by spitting at them, calling them names or throwing things at them. Therefore, the symbol made it easier for Jews to be discriminated against.

A

Jews were made to wear Star of David badges

OVER TO YOU

1 With a partner, draw two different mind maps starting from the concepts of prejudice and discrimination.

2 Why do you think the Nazis discriminated against Jewish people?

3 What other examples do you know of where religious people have been discriminated against?

4 With a partner, produce a *What I can do against discrimination* chart. It might include, for example, 'I will not laugh at anti-religious jokes.'

As the Second World War went on, the Nazi leadership decided it should kill all Jews. It called this the 'Final Solution'. All over Europe, Jews were rounded up and those that were not shot straight away were taken – men, women and children – to **concentration camps**. Here, millions were gassed, shot or starved to death. The result of Hitler's plan was that between six million and seven million Jewish men, women and children had been murdered by the time Germany was defeated in 1945. This is known as the **Holocaust**.

OVER TO YOU

5 Design a memorial to express your feelings about the Holocaust. It can be with words in the form of a poem, an illustration or a model. You could design it to link with Holocaust Remembrance Day.

6 Discuss with a partner what your feelings are when you read that Anna Bergman cannot forgive. Discuss whether you think you would be able to forgive. Give your reasons.

Anna Bergman is a Jewish survivor of the Holocaust who lives in Cardiff today. She was born in Czechoslovakia and lived in Prague. In 1941, she was taken with her husband to a transit centre where people worked for the Nazis. They were separated into male and female barracks, had very little food and many were shot in public. In 1944, she and her husband were taken from the camp. It was the last she saw of him.

She ended up in Auschwitz, a death camp. She was only there for ten days, but long enough to suffer the severe cold and a starvation diet, and to smell the fumes coming from the tall towers. From there, she was taken to Dresden to work in an arms factory.

Next stop was a journey on a train wagon to the concentration camp at Mutthausen in Austria. There, her baby was born – weighing only three pounds. Anna herself was only five stone.

After the Americans liberated the camp, she ended up marrying an RAF officer and went to Cardiff. At the age of 87, she says she can never forgive those who did this to her and her family to the day she dies.

Anna Bergman

For some people alive today who survived the Holocaust, what happened is still too painful to talk about. However, most people agree that we should all remember what happened in the Holocaust, and make sure it never happens again.

Every year on Holocaust Remembrance Day (Yom Hashoah), people remember the Holocaust. The worldwide Jewish community offers prayers for those who died. A permanent memorial called **Yad Vashem** has been set up in Jerusalem. It holds records of all the millions of victims, called the Hall of Names, and also has exhibitions, documents and artefacts from the Holocaust.

The Hall of Names

WEBLINKS You will find links for this topic at
www.nelsonthornes.com/exploringre

How should we treat other people?

This is about ...

- **Identifying and considering times when you have been treated unfairly**
- **Exploring religious teachings on how you should treat other people**
- **Exploring and evaluating the experiences of other people**

Key questions

- **What does it feel like to be treated unfairly?**
- **What is equality?**
- **What do religions teach about equality?**

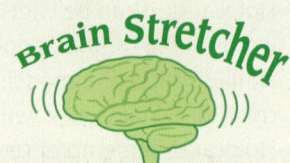

KEY WORDS

- Discrimination
- Equality
- Golden Rule
- Parable
- Prejudice

1 How many times have we said 'It's not fair' because we have been treated in a different way from someone else?

a Give some examples of times when you feel you have been treated unequally.

b How important do you think it is that people are treated the same, no matter what? Why?

All the major world religions teach their followers that everyone should be treated equally no matter where they come from, what they look like or what they believe. Treating people equally means we all have the same opportunities to do things in life, and we all get treated the same. This is an important value that all religions agree on. All religions suggest that we should treat people as we would like to be treated. It is called the **Golden Rule**.

Brain Stretcher

'There is no Greek or Jew, man or woman ... for you are all one in Christ Jesus.'

What do you think this teaching from the Bible means?

A

Hinduism
This is the sum of duty: do not do to others what would cause pain if done to you.
(Mahabharata 5:1517)

Judaism
What is hateful to you, do not do to your fellow man. This is the law: all the rest is commentary.
(Talmud Shabbat 31a)

Christianity
Do for others what you want them to do for you.
(Matthew 7:12)

Buddhism
Hurt not others in ways that you yourself would find hurtful.
(UdanaVarga 5:1)

Sikhism
No one is my enemy, none a stranger and everyone is my friend.
(Guru Granth Sahib 1299)

Islam
None of you 'truly' believe, until you wish for your brothers and sisters what you wish for yourself.
(Hadith)

How does this cartoon show the parable of the good Samaritan?

Jesus used stories called **parables** to teach people how to treat others. He said we should live together on earth as if everyone were neighbours.

Jesus told the parable of the good Samaritan to help people understand this idea better. In the story, Jesus's hero was a person of mixed race whose people, the Samaritans, suffered a lot of **prejudice** and **discrimination** from other tribes. This unlikely person was the one whom Jesus used as his example of a good neighbour.

To read the full story, look in the Bible at Luke 10:25–37.

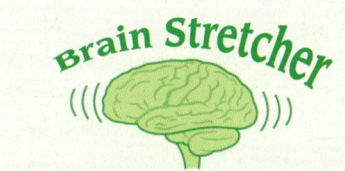

Which of our 'neighbours' in the world today are being treated unfairly? Find a picture to illustrate your choice, maybe from a newspaper or magazine. Explain what is happening to them, and how you could be a 'good Samaritan' and help them.

Help!

Spider diagrams

This is when a main idea (the body of the spider) is explored further (spider legs).

OVER TO YOU

2 Choose one of the following words, and say why you think it best describes the idea behind (a) the Golden Rule and (b) the parable of the good Samaritan.

  a Compassionate: feeling sympathy for others when they are suffering and wanting to do something to help.

  b Helpful: giving assistance or being useful.

  c Thoughtful: showing concern for the needs of others.

  d Kind: being generous, friendly or sympathetic towards others.

3 Write your own parable to explain the meaning of the Golden Rule. You can use one of the ideas below if you wish.

  a At the football game.

  b In the school playground.

  c On the bus into town.

  d The lost purse/pay packet/pension book.

Plan your ideas first as a spider diagram, and then write your parable in no more than 300 words.

How can we see equality in action? Hajj

This is about ...

- Expressing your own ideas of equality
- Understanding how people are seen as equal in the Muslim faith
- Appreciating the experience of equality on Hajj

Key questions

- What examples of **equality** in society do I know of?
- How can people be equal in religion?
- How does being treated equally make people feel?

OVER TO YOU

1 Make a list of examples of people being treated unequally. You can use examples from real life, or maybe from a television programme you have seen.

Muslims believe that when Allah created all living things, all people were created equal.

A

> Allah created the whole world from one soul, ... and that he created everyone with variation in your language and colour.
> (Surah 31)

Even though we might all look or sound different, this is not important. All Muslims consider themselves part of a bigger **community** than just the local ones they live in. This community is called the **ummah**. It is the worldwide community of believers in Islam.

The teaching that all people are equal is seen clearly in the annual **pilgrimage** called **Hajj**. This pilgrimage is something all Muslims who are physically and financially able must do at least once in their lifetime.

Fantastic Facts

Hajj is a truly amazing event!
- More than two million pilgrims attend Hajj each year.
- Pilgrims come to Hajj from over 150 countries.
- Pilgrims stay in 44,000 air-conditioned tents.
- 50 million bags of ice and cool water are given out to pilgrims each year.

B

C

2 Read Yusuf's first experience of Hajj when he was 15. Identify the parts of his experience where you can see people being equal.

Yusuf

Nothing could have prepared me for the sight that met us when we first arrived in the holy city of **Makkah**. *I couldn't believe how many Muslim brothers and sisters there were. Everywhere you looked, there were thousands upon thousands of men and women, all colours and all speaking different languages. My father told me that in total there were probably about two million* **pilgrims** *from all around the world here for Hajj.*

Then we began the rituals and journey of Hajj. Everyone dressed in the pilgrim's clothes of **ihram**, *which is a white garment. You spend all of Hajj in ihram, which symbolises that you are cleansing your soul of sin. The sight of two million Muslims all dressed in ihram was really special. When it came to prayer, the noise of all of us praising Allah in Arabic was something I'll always hear and remember. When I was standing, shoulder to shoulder with my eyes shut in prayer with African,*

American and other Muslims, all I could hear was one voice together – no accents or different languages.

For the rest of the 11 days on pilgrimage, we all moved together, slept in the same tents and shared the same food. It was easy to forget where I was from, and being British or Welsh or Asian was unimportant during Hajj, because I was a Muslim there, the same as everyone else. It was the most fantastic experience of my life. It taught me a lot about looking beyond people's appearances and differences, which I often see people fail to do at home in Rhyl and at school. Muhammad (peace be upon him) once said, 'All of you descend from Adam', and on Hajj it really felt like we were all one because we shared the same beliefs and values. Nobody is more important than anyone else.

D

Scenes from Hajj

3 Complete the following tasks through small group discussions:

a Make a list of the positive experiences that Yusuf had while on Hajj.

b What difference do you think wearing ihram makes to a pilgrim?

c What has Yusuf learned about the meaning of equality by going on Hajj?

4 On your own, complete this evaluation:

Muslims believe going on Hajj is an important way to learn about equality because…

5 You can get some idea of the Hajj experience by going to the virtual Hajj pages from the weblinks suggested. Compare the virtual tour with Yusuf's account. What similarities and differences can you find?

 **You will find links for this topic at**
www.nelsonthornes.com/exploringre

How do we make things change? (1) Martin Luther King

This is about ...

- **Studying and evaluating the lives of people who have challenged inequality in the world**

OVER TO YOU

1. What do you understand by the term 'inequality'? Try to come to a definition in the class.

2. Work with a partner. Produce a mind map starting with the word inequality.

3. With the same partner, make a list of things you would like to see changed in the world because they are examples of inequality. They might have appeared in your mind map. Rank them in order of importance.

Key questions

- What **inequalities** do I want changed in the world?
- What can people do to change things?
- Who has inspired change in the past?

KEY WORDS

- Direct action
- Discrimination
- Inequality
- Segregation

Help!

Mind map

A mind map starts with a main idea or topic at the centre of a page with branches to sub topics which branch out further again. Use drawings and colours as well as writing the connections along the branches.

Until the 1960s, some laws in parts of the USA meant black people were discriminated against. White and black children were not taught together in schools, and there was **segregation** (separation) between black and white people on public transport, on beaches, and in shops and cafés. White people got the best schools, the best seats on the bus and the best service in shops. Very importantly, black citizens in these US states did not have the right to vote, which meant they could not get any of these discriminating laws changed.

As a black American, Dr Martin Luther King Junior had suffered from **discrimination** himself. As a Christian, he believed treating people unfairly because of the colour of their skin was against Jesus's teaching of love your neighbour. So, in 1956, he began joining in with campaigns against any treatment that discriminated against black people.

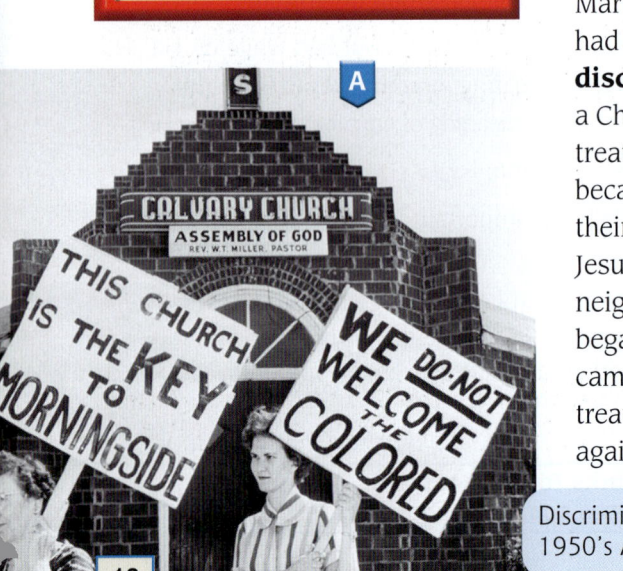

A

Discrimination in 1950's America

B

Dr Martin Luther King

He took **direct action**, organising boycotts of public transport like the buses. This meant black people stopped using the buses until they were allowed to sit anywhere they wanted – it was very successful as it was costing the bus companies a lot of money. Also, he organised sit-ins and demonstrations, led several peace marches where he was joined by millions of black and white people from across America, and made many important speeches against racial discrimination.

Despite often being arrested, having his house bombed and being stabbed, Dr King knew that God's love was always with him. This made him determined to carry on fighting for equal rights. He was shot dead on 4 April 1968. He was only 39 years old, but had achieved so much because of his determination to act on his beliefs. By the time he was assassinated, black people in America no longer had to be segregated from white citizens and had gained the right to vote.

You can still read his speeches today, and they are so powerful that they continue to inspire the work of people against all types of inequalities in the world.

Fantastic Facts

- In 1964, Martin Luther King was awarded the Nobel Peace Prize for his protest against discrimination – the youngest person to have been awarded this great prize.
- His name was changed to Martin when he was six. Before that he had been called Michael!
- His 'I have a dream' speech was voted the greatest speech of the twentieth century.

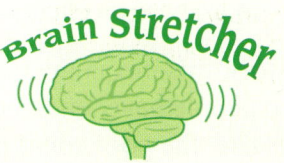

OVER TO YOU

4   Why do you think Martin Luther King is still an inspirational role model for people all over the world, nearly 50 years after his death?

5   Martin Luther King was born in 1929. If he had not been assassinated, he might still be alive today, in his late seventies.

   a   If you could meet him today, what five questions would you ask him?

   b   Why do you want to know the answers?

6   Your teacher will show you some pictures of the direct action taken by Martin Luther King and his supporters, or you can listen to one of his speeches. Do some stilling and meditation on this.

Brain Stretcher

In the parable of the good Samaritan, the only one who helped the traveller was the Samaritan, a man who had been discriminated against all his life. The priest and the Levite, both 'good people', passed by. Dr King once said: 'We will have to repent in this generation not merely for the vitriolic [poisonous] words and actions of the bad people, but for the appalling silence of the good people.'

What do you think Dr King meant by this? Who were the 'good people'?

In what way do you think Dr King was inspired by the parable of the good Samaritan? Give some evidence from Dr King's actions to end discrimination in your answer.

Help!

Stilling and meditation
Stilling is simply to be still and relaxed and meditation is to concentrate on something to help you think more deeply.

WEBLINKS You will find links for this topic at www.nelsonthornes.com/exploringre

How do we make things change? (2) Mahatma Gandhi

This is about ...

- Studying and evaluating the lives of people who have challenged inequality in the world

Key questions

- What **inequalities** do I want changed in the world?
- What can people do to change things?
- Who has inspired change in the past?

KEY WORDS

- Ahimsa
- Caste
- Direct action
- Harijan
- Inequality
- Prejudice

Why are some people rich and others poor? This is a big question, and there are many different answers. Where you live in the world, the jobs your parents have, the education you get, the government you vote for, how hard you work or even whether you just have good luck – all these things and many more have an effect.

Throughout history, this inequality between rich and poor has always existed. The rich people have tended to like the situation as it is. They have said things like 'the poor could be rich too if they worked harder', or 'God wishes some people to be rich and some poor', or 'it is an economic law that not everyone can be rich'.

But the poor have not always seen things in this way. People have pointed out that rich people, and rich countries, tend to organise things so that they stay rich, and get richer, at the expense of the poor.

Fantastic Facts

The name 'Mahatma' was given to Gandhi as a title of respect. It means 'Great Soul'. His actual name was Mohandas Gandhi.

Mumbai, India

OVER TO YOU

1. Look at photo **A** of poor people in Mumbai, India.

    a   How do you know these are poor people?

    b   What do you think can be done for them and who might be able to do it?

    c   What do you think the slogans painted on the walls are protesting about?

Traditionally in India, there have been different roles given to different people in society, for example priests or soldiers. Many Hindus believe you are born into your role, or **caste**, as a result of your actions in past lives. This has often lead to **prejudice** between castes, especially towards the poorest in society.

The poorest people of all were called untouchables. They were seen as being below any caste at all. They were given the dirtiest jobs and were not allowed to mix with other castes in the villages and temples.

Gandhi took **direct action** and set about campaigning for equal rights for all Hindus, regardless of caste. He always tried to help untouchables and renamed them **harijans**, meaning 'children of God'. In 1948, the Indian government passed a law to abolish untouchability.

Gandhi also campaigned for an end to British rule in India, and was a very important part in making this happen. His own behaviour set an example and inspired many to do the same.

Mahatma Gandhi

It is better to die than to give in to bad laws. We won't fight with guns and swords and we won't hate the white government. But we will not do as they tell us any more.

(Gandhi)

Gandhi believed strongly in the Hindu code of **ahimsa**, which means 'having reverence for all life'. He believed in non-violent protest as a way of challenging inequality. Thousands joined him in his campaigns.

He believed that inequality could be overcome by returning hatred with love, disrespect with respect, and refusing to give in to mistreatment.

OVER TO YOU

2 Treating people equally is an important value that all religions agree on. In what way do you think Gandhi showed this value?

3 **a** If you could meet Gandhi today, what five questions would you ask him?

b Why do you want to know the answers?

4 What would you take direct action against today? List the kind of things you could do, and how they would make a difference. Remember that Gandhi believed in ahimsa and non-violent protest.

5 When you have finished your evaluations, make a small group with other people. Share your ideas and present them in a way that can be displayed to the class, e.g. a poster with the information, or as a newspaper article or a leaflet.

Brain Stretcher

Gandhi renamed the untouchables as the children of God. Do you think the labels we give groups make a difference? Give examples from your own experiences.

How do we make things change?
(3) The Dalai Lama

This is about ...

■ Studying and evaluating the lives of people who have challenged inequality in the world

Key questions

■ What **inequalities** do I want changed in the world?

■ What can people do to change things?

■ Who has inspired change in the past?

How do we challenge inequality in the world today? There are powerful countries in the modern world who have huge armies, nuclear weapons and massive economic power. If you live in a small, poor country, what can you do to stand up against **oppression** by a big, rich and powerful country?

Fantastic Facts

• Before he was recognised by the holy men, the Dalai Lama's name was Lhamo Thondup.

• There are now more Chinese people living in Tibet than Tibetan people.

KEY WORDS

• Direct action
• Discrimination
• Inequality
• Monastery
• Noble Eightfold Path
• Oppression
• Reincarnation

The Dalai Lama is a religious and political leader from Tibet, a small, mountainous country near China. He is a Buddhist. When he was two years old, he was recognised by holy men as the fourteenth **reincarnation** of the first Dalai Lama, and he began many years of training to be the leader of his country.

A   The Dalai Lama

OVER TO YOU

1 What great leaders do you know about, either dead or alive? Make a list of them. Which of them are religious? In pairs, discuss each one of them and decide how much influence they have had and what kind of influence it was. Give each one a score from 1 to 5 (1 is the highest).

2 Study photo **A**, which shows the Dalai Lama addressing a large crowd.

a Where in the world do you think this photo might have been taken?

b There are thousands of people in the audience. Why might they have come to see the Dalai Lama speak? Write down two or three possibilities.

c Have you ever been in a large crowd like this? Can you imagine speaking to such a huge crowd? What would it feel like? Write a few lines for your answer.

B The Noble Eightfold Path

Step 1 Right vision – try to see things as they really are: nothing lasts forever

Step 2 Right emotion – try to have a positive attitude: thinking good of people

Step 3 Right speech – try to tell the truth: avoid gossip and hurtful words

Step 4 Right action – try to do the right thing: not to harm others or steal or be rude, speak the truth, respect your body

Step 5 Right livelihood – try to do work that helps others rather than harming living things

Step 6 Right effort – try to think first about what you say or do

Step 7 Right awareness – try to always be aware of what you do and how it affects others

Step 8 Right concentration – try to use meditation to reach a higher level of understanding

For many years, the people of Tibet have been suffering because of **discrimination** by the Chinese government. Chinese forces invaded Tibet in 1950, and in the years following a Tibetan uprising in 1959 they destroyed nearly all of Tibet's 6,000 Buddhist **monasteries** and killed about 1.2 million Buddhist followers.

It is too dangerous for many Tibetan Buddhists to worship openly and far too dangerous for the Dalai Lama to live there.

He escaped from Tibet in 1959 and has never been able to return to his country. Since 1994, the Chinese government has ordered that all evidence of the Dalai Lama be removed from people's homes and temples.

By following a central part of the Buddha's teachings, called the **Noble Eightfold Path**, all Buddhists try to live in a considerate way towards others.

Since his exile from Tibet, the Dalai Lama has taken **direct action**, working to help the people of his country and make their troubles known. He continually travels the world, making others aware of the Tibetan people and their problems through speeches and worship. For his work he has won the Nobel Peace Prize.

3 Look at the Noble Eightfold Path in box **B**. Think of some examples of the following today: right speech, right action and right livelihood? How do you think the Dalai Lama's work against inequality fits with each of these three steps?

4 **a** If you could meet the Dalai Lama today, what five questions would you ask him?

   b Why do you want to know the answers?

5 What would you take direct action against today? List the kind of things you could do, and how they would make a difference. Remember that Buddhists try never to harm others.

6 When you have finished your evaluations, make a small group with other people. Share your ideas and present them in a way that can be displayed to the class, e.g. a poster with the information, or as a newspaper article or a leaflet.

Is everyone special?

This is about ...

- Exploring how worship in Sikhism allows followers to be equal
- Considering sharing
- Examining the role of women in the Sikh faith

Key questions

- Do I live in an equal way with others?
- How does Sikhism practise **equality** through worship?
- Why is equality important?

OVER TO YOU

1 Who does most of the work in your house? Make a list of the jobs that need doing and who does them.

2 Look back at your answers to task 1 on page 6. When you thought about the people who were in each job, did you tend to think of them as being men or women?

3 Look at photos **A–C**. Write down what you can see about the men and women from the different pictures. Who is leading the service? Where are the men and women sitting? Who or what looks the most important thing in each picture?

KEY WORDS

- Discrimination
- Equality
- Five Ks
- Gurdwara
- Gurmukhi
- Guru
- Guru Granth Sahib
- Guru Nanak
- Khalsa
- Langar

Religious ceremonies in places of worship

OVER TO YOU

4 Read Davinder's account of worship in the **gurdwara**. Once you have finished, make a list of things that show men and women do the same things in worship, and a list of the things they do differently.

The Langar

Discrimination can mean that people are treated badly because of their colour, because they are poor, because they are not powerful and important. People are also often discriminated against because they are women. All over the world, it is men who have the best jobs, who have power and influence, who tell women what to do and how to behave. It is only recently that this started to change in the UK.

The fair treatment of women is a big part of Sikh beliefs, as **Guru Nanak** taught this more than 450 years ago. He said that even the most powerful man would not exist if not for his mother giving him life. In Sikh history, many women have fought alongside men. They are allowed to join the **Khalsa** in exactly the same way as men and to wear the **Five Ks**. Some female Khalsa members wear a turban as the men do.

As soon as we enter the gurdwara, everyone takes off their shoes and washes their hands. My family always take an offering for the **Guru Granth Sahib**. My brother and I take turns in giving it, but we all kneel and bow our heads to the floor in respect before we sit down on the floor.

Davinder

There aren't any special places to sit, but men and women sit on different sides. I once asked my mum why this happens, and she said it was not a religious teaching that had to be followed, just that it was an Indian custom from the old days because it made it easier to worship.

Everyone sits on the floor to be lower than the **Guru**. This is a sign of respect, as we believe the holy book is just like all the other living Gurus and should be treated in a special way. Sitting like this also reminds us of the first community of Sikhs in Anandpur, which Guru Nanak set up and where everyone lived together, ate together and praised God together.

During worship, we will listen to readings from the Guru Granth Sahib, sing hymns, pray and meditate. After worship, we go back downstairs to the **langar** hall to share a meal. This is a free kitchen where anyone can have a meal. There is no charge for the food and you can sit where you like.

OVER TO YOU

5 Guru Nanak said: 'Men and women are all equal before God.' Yet men and women are not always treated the same. Write a list of some ways in which you think women or men are treated unfairly in the world today.

Faith • Faith • Faith CONNECTIONS

Sikhism states there is one God. Photo **E** is a Sikh symbol made up of the words 'there is one' written in **Gurmukhi**. Find out what other religions teach about the 'oneness' of God, and make a collage poster of sayings. What symbols can you find from different religions about God as One? Add them to your collage and design your own.

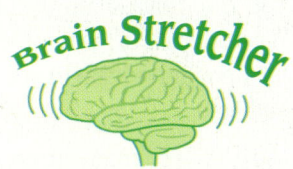

Brain Stretcher

When Guru Nanak said that women were equal with men and should share in worship, this was shocking to some people of his time. What might Guru Nanak think about our society today? Do you think he would be happy with what he saw?

23

Stereotyping, prejudice and discrimination

Our journey

In our journey through this unit, we have:

- discussed the meanings of stereotyping, prejudice and discrimination
- explored different ways in which people are stereotyped
- investigated ways in which people have been discriminated against for their beliefs, or because they are black, poor, powerless or female
- explored and evaluated leaders who have taken direct action against discrimination and inequality, and the beliefs that influenced them
- expressed our own views on stereotyping, prejudice and discrimination

Many people throughout history have acted to challenge **prejudice** and **discrimination**. In this unit we have evaluated the work of Martin Luther King, Mahatma Gandhi and the Dalai Lama. For these three people, their religious order influenced the path they took in life.

Of course, it is not only people with religious beliefs who challenge prejudice and discrimination. However, because all the main religions have such strong messages about how people should treat each other, religion has made a big difference. On the other hand, people have also discriminated against others because of their religion.

Key question

- **How can I challenge prejudice and discrimination within my community?**

How could your school do more to tackle prejudice and discrimination? Design an anti-discrimination poster for display on school noticeboards or to take to your school council for discussion.

You could tackle a particular issue – like attitudes to disability, race or poverty – or you could design something that challenges an issue in your school, such as bullying or name-calling.

We all see so many images each day that it is difficult to grab people's attention. Here are some tips on what makes for a successful poster campaign:

a   Have a simple message that's quick to read.
b   Use attention-grabbing, exciting words.
c   Use striking colours and images.
d   Involve your audience: ask questions, challenge beliefs.
e   Know your audience: what do they like, trust, believe? Use that to get your message across.

In groups, brainstorm ways to grab your audience's attention.

KEY WORDS

- **Direct action**
- **Discrimination**
- **Inequality**
- **Prejudice**
- **Stereotype**

You could use a quote from a famous person in your poster. People tend to trust messages from people they know of and respect. Here are some quotes about **direct action** that you could use to inspire your audience.

Christopher Reeve

Don't give up. Don't lose hope. Don't sell out.

Do not wait for leaders; do it alone, person to person.

Mother Teresa

You must be the change you wish to see in the world.

Mahatma Gandhi

If you are neutral in situations of injustice, you have chosen the side of the oppressor. If an elephant has its foot on the tail of a mouse and you say you are neutral, the mouse will not appreciate your neutrality.

Archbishop Desmond Tutu

If you want to make peace with your enemy, you have to work with your enemy. Then he becomes your partner.

How wonderful it is that nobody needs to wait a single moment before starting to improve the world.

The time is always right to do what is right.

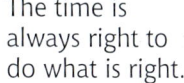

Anne Frank

Martin Luther King

Nelson Mandela

Reality is wrong. Dreams are for real.

Pop music tells you that everything is OK and rock music tells you that it's not, but that you can change it.

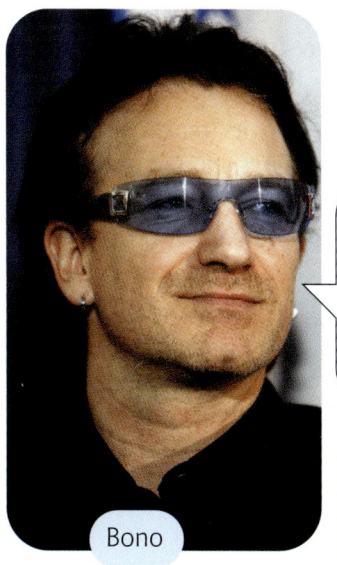

If you put the hard work in, you have a chance of fulfilling your dream.

Tanni Grey-Thompson

Bono

Tupac Shakur

This is about ...

- Considering what is meant by the idea of freedom
- Exploring and reflecting on different ideas about being free
- Evaluating whether or not everyone in the world is free
- Investigating situations where people do not have their freedom
- Exploring religious teachings on freedom, and how these teachings have influenced people to fight for freedom

Key questions

- What is **freedom**?
- How free am I?
- Is everyone free?

KEY WORDS

- Freedom

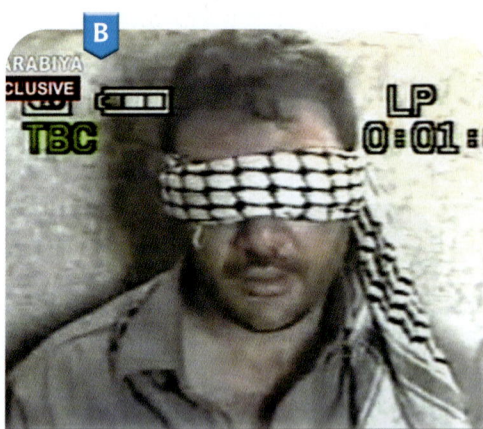

A famous American president, Franklin D Roosevelt, said there were four freedoms:

1   Freedom of speech and expression, everywhere in the world.

2   Freedom of everyone to worship God in his own way, everywhere in the world.

3   Freedom from want, everywhere in the world.

4   Freedom from fear, anywhere in the world.

OVER TO YOU

1   a   In what way do you agree with Franklin D Roosevelt?

   b   What other freedoms can you think of?

2   What do you think the world would be like if everyone were free to do whatever they wanted?

3   a   In pairs, make a list of the things you are free to do.

   b   Then make another list of the things you are not free to do.

   c   Look at your lists and decide whether it is right that you are free or not free to do each of the things you have written down.

4 Look at pictures **A–D**. When people are not allowed to do certain things, we sometimes say they are being denied their freedom. What freedoms are these people being denied? What would need to be done so they could have their freedom?

5 Produce a concept map on the theme of 'freedom'. Here are some words to use in it, which you should copy onto separate cards.

JUSTICE   WEALTH

IMPRISONMENT

POVERTY   HEALTH

HAPPINESS   ADDICTION

HOPE   DEATH   WAR

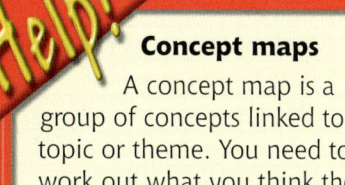

Help!

Concept maps

A concept map is a group of concepts linked to a topic or theme. You need to work out what you think the links and relationships are. Draw lines between the words and write on them what you think the links are.

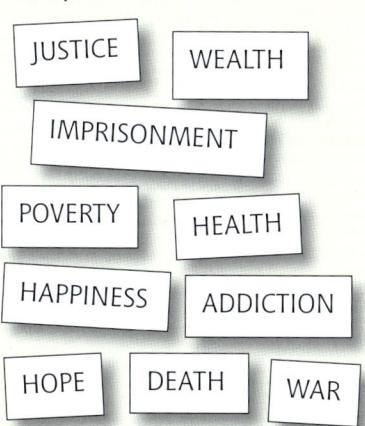

E *When we let freedom ring, we let it ring from every village and every hamlet, from every state and every city, we will be able to speed up that day when all of God's children, black men and white men, Jews and gentiles, Protestants and Catholics, will be able to join hands and sing in the words of the old Negro spiritual: 'Free at last! Free at last! Thank God Almighty, we are free at last!'*

Martin Luther King

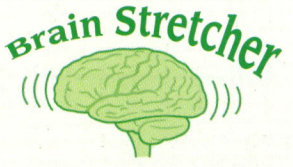

6 Read the words in box **E**. What Christian ideas do you see there?

7 What kind of freedom did Martin Luther King dream about?

8 Why did he think freedom was so important?

Brain Stretcher

'There is a wonderful mythical law of nature that the three things we crave most in life – happiness, freedom and peace of mind – are always attained by giving them to someone else' (Peyton Conway March, American general, 1864–1955).

In what ways do you think this is true?

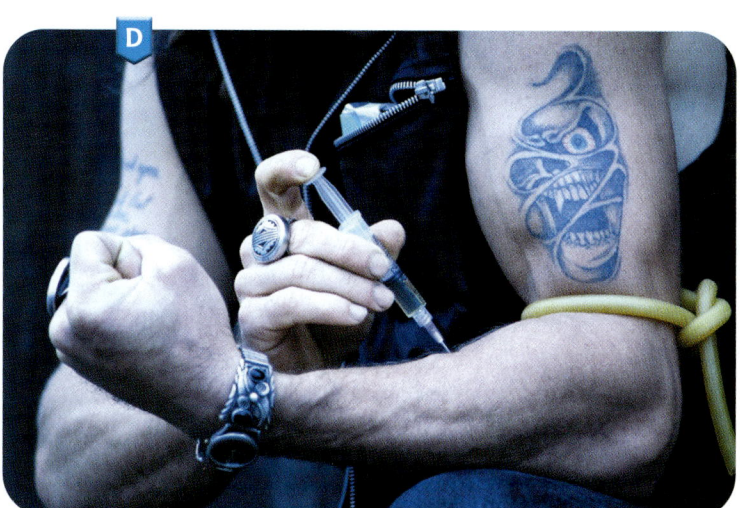

D

Are we really free?

This is about ...

- **Discussing whether or not you are completely free to live your life as you want**
- **Exploring religious theories about choice**

Islam, Judaism and Christianity teach that when God created human beings, he gave them **free will**. This means that everyone has free choice in their lives over what they do. Everyone is responsible for their own actions. Sometimes, however, it might not feel like we have free choice. There always seem to be rules about what we can and cannot do.

KEY WORDS

- **Free will**
- **Karma**
- **Qur'an**
- **Torah**
- **Unjust**

B

1. I can buy any food I want.
2. I can stay home from school whenever I want if I do not like the lessons I will be having that day.
3. I can watch all my favourite programmes on television.
4. I can get up when I want.
5. I can stay up until whatever time I want.
6. I can go where I like on holiday.
7. I can wear any clothes I want.
8. I can say whatever I like.
9. I can eat what I like.
10. I can read what I like.

Key questions

- **Am I really free to make my own choices about my life?**
- **What are the consequences of my choices?**

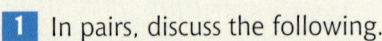

1 In pairs, discuss the following.

   a List three choices you know you can make in your life.
   b Which parts of our lives do we control?
   c In what way do you think we are able to decide what our future will be?

2 a Read the statements in box **B**. In pairs, discuss what kind of choice is involved in the statements. Use a large copy of the table below and tick the column that applies to each statement.

Statement	Free choice	Some choice	No choice
1			
2			
3			
4			
5			
6			
7			
8			
9			
10			

   b Which statements were free choices?

3 What would the world be like if we could always do what we wanted or always have our own way?

4 Discuss whether freedom is a good or a bad thing using the + – ? method. List your ideas under the three headings.

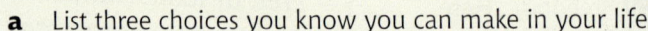

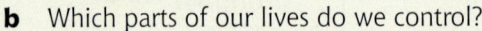

+ – ?

+ stands for what is good about it
– stands for what is bad about it
? stands for what you are not sure about

Adam and Eve disobeyed God when they ate fruit from the tree of knowledge

The story of God giving free will can be found in the beginning of three sacred texts: the Bible, the **Torah** and the **Qur'an**. This story tells how Adam and Eve disobeyed God's rules and did something they were not supposed to do. God told them not to eat the fruit of the tree that contained the knowledge of all things in the world. However, they were tempted to go against God, and so they did what they wanted – they ate the fruit. From that point on, their relationship with God changed. Human beings now had the power to make the world a fair and just place, following God's rules, or to make it unfair and **unjust**, going against God's will.

Christians, Jews and Muslims also believe God will judge everyone on how they have behaved when they were alive, and what choices they made – good and bad. Therefore, even though the consequences of our choices are not always immediately obvious, these religions teach that at some point in the future we will be judged on the choices we have made.

OVER TO YOU

5 Look at the cartoons in picture **D**, which show situations when people are upset.
For each cartoon, discuss:
   a   What bad choice do you think has been made?
   b   What will be the consequences?
   c   How can the situation be resolved?

6 Read the story of the fall in Genesis in the Bible, Genesis 3. Complete a storyboard of the key events.

7 When have you made a bad choice? What happened? How did you feel?

In Hinduism, how people act in their present life affects what happens to them in their next life. The word **karma** means action, and just as you can build up a balance of money in the bank, Hindus believe they build up a balance of good or bad karma to take to their next lives. If you start a new life with bad karma from the past, there is no point in complaining – you are responsible for the hard and difficult life you have entered. The best way to develop good karma for future lives is for everyone to live properly and do their duty as completely and as well as possible.

Help!

Storyboards
A storyboard is a visual way of telling a story. You can use a combination of flow charts, drawings, photos and text to show what happens, scene by scene.

OVER TO YOU

8 Why might a Hindu say there is no point in complaining about life being unfair?

9 How would the teaching of karma affect the way Hindus live?

How do people cope with captivity?

This is about ...

- **Understanding why Christians would want to help a hostage situation**
- **Exploring how two Christians coped with their loss of freedom**

Key questions

- **Can someone be free while in captivity?**
- **Why did these two Christians act as they did?**
- **What can I do to make sure everyone is free?**

KEY WORDS

- **Archbishop**
- **Captivity**
- **Communist**
- **Evangelical**
- **Freedom**
- **Hostage**
- **Responsibility**

Protests for the release of hostages in Iraq

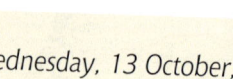

Wednesday, 13 October, 2004

BAGHDAD, Iraq (CNN) – The United States tried twice to rescue the two Americans and one British citizen held hostage in Iraq, according to a US official with direct knowledge of the attempts.

From CNN News (www.CNN.com)

Terry Waite

Terry Waite, working as a special member of the **Archbishop** of Canterbury's team, went to Beirut in the Middle East in January 1987. He went to negotiate the release of several hostages being held there. However, he ended up a hostage himself and was held captive for 1,760 days before being released on 18 November 1991. Terry Waite wrote the following about his imprisonment.

I had no contact at all with my family for five years – they didn't know that I was alive or dead for about four years ... I was in solitary confinement and I used to communicate with hostages in the cell next door by tapping on the wall in code.

I remember saying to myself after I was taken hostage, 'No regrets – you haven't done everything correctly, you're bound to have made mistakes, but stick by what you've done; no self pity – don't begin to feel sorry for yourself, there are loads of people who are in worse situations than yourself.'

Over recent years, you might have seen examples on the news of a number of **hostage** situations. People are often taken hostage for political reasons. Those holding them use the lives of hostages to bargain with. People are often taken hostage very quickly. One minute they are leading a normal life, the next they are being held captive, their life in the balance. Some hostages have been released, while others have been killed by the people holding them.

1 Try to imagine being held hostage as Terry Waite was. What kinds of emotions do you think he experienced?

2 Do you think the fact that Terry Waite was working for the Church made any difference to his experiences? Explain your views.

3 Why do you think Christians such as the Archbishop of Canterbury and Terry Waite decided to become involved in dangerous situations like this? Explore the following passages from the Bible to get some ideas:

   a Luke 4:16–19.
   b Matthew 25:31–46.
   c Matthew 22:34–40.
   d Hebrews 13:1–3.

Richard Wurmbrand was an **evangelical** Christian minister who spent 14 years in **Communist** imprisonment and torture in Romania.

When the Communists came to power, they tried to take control of the churches. Richard Wurmbrand refused to co-operate and began an 'underground' ministry to his people and the invading Russian soldiers. After he was arrested in 1948, he spent three years alone in a cell, where he was beaten, starved and tortured. In May 1966, Richard Wurmbrand told his story to the American government. Stripping to the waist, he revealed 18 deep torture marks.

Yet he never stopped loving and praising God. In his books and sermons, he says it is possible to be free even when in prison. He felt he had a different kind of **freedom**. Because of his faith, he felt he was a free man even when he was locked up, tortured and starved.

4 Produce a living graph of the events in Richard Wurmbrand's life. You could include some of the following: he refused to co-operate; his underground ministry; he was arrested and placed in solitary confinement; he was beaten and starved; he was later released and gave account to the American court.

5 Why might Christians like Richard Wurmbrand believe it is possible to be free when suffering and behind bars? Use these Bible passages to help you:

   a Romans 8:1–2.
   b Galatians 5:1.
   c John 8:36.
   d Philippians 1:12–18.

6 Has your study of Terry Waite and Richard Wurmbrand altered your view of what it is to be free? Explain what you mean.

Brain Stretcher

'Freedom means **responsibility**. That is why most people dread it' (George Bernard Shaw, Irish playwright, 1856–1950).

What do you think he meant? Do you agree with him?

7 'Taking a hostage can never be right.' Do you agree? Explain your views.

8 Imagine you are Richard Wurmbrand. Write a letter to the religious leaders in the UK explaining what has happened to you, the decisions you made and why you made them.

 **You will find links for this topic at** www.nelsonthornes.com/exploringre

Why is Pesach about freedom?

This is about ...

- **Understanding that the festival of Pesach is about freedom**
- **Empathising with Anne Frank and her loss of freedom**

Key questions

- Why do Jews think **Pesach** is important?
- How do Jews cope with suffering?

KEY WORDS

- **Freedom**
- **Haggadah**
- **Holocaust**
- **Pesach**
- **Pharaoh**
- **Seder**

Sarah and her family have come together to celebrate the **seder** meal as part of the festival of Pesach. Let her tell you what it is all about. She knows the story well because every year during the festival of Pesach her family retell the story to remember the time Jews spent in captivity and how God helped them to become free.

Celebrating the seder meal

Sarah

Pesach is a holiday for Jewish people. It reminds them of the time when Jews were freed from slavery in the land of Egypt. They were slaves, and they wanted to be free. Moses tried to get the **Pharaoh** *to free the Jewish slaves, but the Pharaoh refused. God had told Moses that if the Pharaoh refused to let his people go, he would send terrible plagues down on the Egyptians. After the tenth plague, the Pharaoh gave in and the Jews fled from their captivity.*

The story is read in a special order from the book called a **Haggadah**, *which means 'to tell'. At the seder meal, our family tells the story of our ancestors, and we remind ourselves that we are now a free people. During the seder, we eat traditional and symbolic foods that remind us of the Jewish people and their suffering through the ages.*

Celebrating Pesach is very special to me and my family because it helps us remember the importance of **freedom** *– not just in our history as Jewish people, but also in more recent times when we suffered in the* **Holocaust**, *and today at times of war and oppression around the world. At the seder meal, Jews celebrate their freedom, but they also remember all those who are not yet free.*

Two items are not eaten:

- A roasted egg – a reminder of the festival sacrifice.
- A roasted lamb bone – this represents the lamb that used to be sacrificed at Pesach.

Four items are eaten:

- Bitter herbs – a reminder of the bitter lives of those in slavery.
- Green vegetables – a reminder that Pesach is a spring festival.
- Haroset (chopped apple, nuts, cinnamon and wine) – this symbolises the cement used by their ancestors to build houses for the Egyptians.
- Salt water – this represents the tears of ancestors.

The seder plate

1 Using the weblinks suggested, carry out some research on the festival of Pesach.

2 In small groups, produce a map from memory of the seder plate.

3 Sarah talks about the symbolic food eaten. Study the seder plate and make a table explaining what the different foods stand for.

4 Why is Pesach called a festival of freedom?

5 Why is this festival important to Jews today?

C

Anne Frank

Born on 12 June 1929 in Frankfurt, Germany, Anne Frank was a Jewish teenager who was forced to go into hiding during the Holocaust. During the Second World War, she and her family, along with four others, spent 25 months in a hidden annexe of rooms above her father's office in the Dutch city of Amsterdam. The annexe was crowded and everyone had to be extremely careful not to be heard or seen. If they were discovered, the Nazis would arrest them. During these two years, Anne kept a diary of her life. One of the last gatherings the Frank family shared with one another before they were captured was Pesach.

Fantastic Facts

The Diary of Anne Frank has been translated into 67 languages and is one of the most widely read books in the world.

Map from memory

To produce a map from memory one member of each group comes to the front, looks at the image for ten seconds, returns to the group and draws what can be remembered. Each member of the group does the same and adds to the collective drawing that emerges from each group.

6 Read some extracts from *The Diary of Anne Frank*.

7 Try to imagine how Anne Frank may have felt at different times of her life. Use a living graph to explore her thoughts and feelings.

8 'I can feel the sufferings of millions and yet, if I look up into the heavens, I think that it will all come right, that this cruelty too will end, and that peace and tranquillity will return again. In the meantime, I must uphold my ideals, for perhaps the time will come when I shall be able to carry them out.' Reflect on these words of Anne Frank in her diary. What do you think they say about her attitude to her loss of freedom?

9 Write an imaginary description of the group of people in the secret annexe celebrating Pesach. Concentrate on how they might be feeling about the present and the future, and explain why.

Living graphs

A living graph has two axes. One is a timeline and the other shows, for example, people's feelings. Often you will be given pieces of 'evidence' such as letters or statements, which are cut out and placed where you think they should go on a blank graph outline.

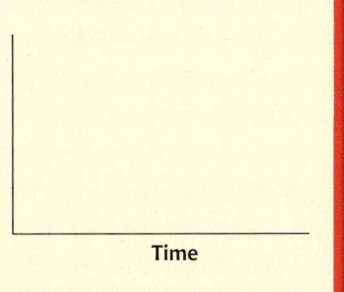

Time

Brain Stretcher

'We all live with the objective of being happy; our lives are all different and yet the same' (Anne Frank).

How much does being happy depend on being free?

WEBLINKS You will find links for this topic at www.nelsonthornes.com/exploringre

What does it mean to act 'justly'?

This is about ...

- Understanding what is meant by the idea of justice
- Exploring examples of justice and injustice
- Investigating ideas of justice from religious perspectives

Key questions

- What is **justice**?
- What is **injustice**?
- Where are there injustices in the world?
- What can we learn about justice from religious teachings?

You could say that the world would be a just place when all people in the world are treated fairly and equally, have their **human rights** given to them and are able to live without suffering or **oppression**. You may have heard the word 'justice' being used to describe a punishment given to someone because of a crime they have committed. In this sense, it means that the punishment received is fair. When people talk about a **just war**, they are describing a war that is taking place under fair rules.

Therefore, anything that is to do with justice is to do with fair treatment. Where fair treatment is not taking place, this is called injustice. When this happens, people's freedoms are taken away from them.

There are many stories of religious leaders fighting for justice. In Islam, the **Prophet Muhammad** is the greatest role model of a just and honest man. It was because of this excellent reputation that he was often asked to make decisions about punishments for crimes, sort out any tribal feuds, and act as a judge in legal and social disputes.

KEY WORDS

- **Community**
- **Conscience**
- **Human rights**
- **Injustice**
- **Just war**
- **Justice**
- **Muhammad**
- **Oppression**
- **Prophet**

1. What kind of things come into your mind when you think of justice? With a partner, draw a mind map exploring the concept of justice.

2. **a** In pairs, list the things you see in society and the world that are not fair or just.

   b For each injustice, suggest how the situation could be made better.

3. Make a list of three things you could do to make the world a fairer and more just place.

A good example of this is the story of a woman from a wealthy and powerful family who was found guilty of theft. Many of the Prophet's followers thought she was too important to be punished, and that the crime should be ignored and forgotten about. However, the Prophet refused to do this and showed anger at the idea, saying, 'Many a **community** ruined itself in the past as they only punished the poor and ignored the crimes of the rich. By Allah, if my own daughter Fatima would have committed theft she would receive the same punishment as a poor stranger or beggar.'

One group of Christians who campaign for prisoners of **conscience** to be freed from imprisonment is called Christians Against Torture (CAT). CAT is a growing voluntary human rights organisation, linked to Amnesty International and working under the umbrella of Cytun (the Council of Churches) in Wales.

Prisoners of conscience are people who have been imprisoned because of their beliefs, even if they have not committed any crime. CAT's aim is to take action against any government that imprisons someone for speaking out against oppression, because this is what Jesus himself did.

On their website, CAT says it is important to help prisoners of conscience because:

- every man, woman and child bears the image of God (Genesis 1:26)
- Jesus proclaims liberty to the captives and freedom to the oppressed, and lists concern for the prisoner among the issues for judgement (Matthew 25:35–40)
- we should be concerned about the conditions in which prisoners are held and the treatment they receive (Hebrews 13:3)
- Jesus himself was tortured to death and he suffers through today's victims. We turn our faces from them at the risk of rejecting him.

Here is what one prisoner, Mehdi Zana, said about the support he received from CAT:

During all those years of torture, persecution and imprisonment, I received many letters from your country … and it was for me a source of courage, brotherhood and moral support … It touched me very much and it touched also my friends in prison.

A

The Angry Christ by Lino Pontebon

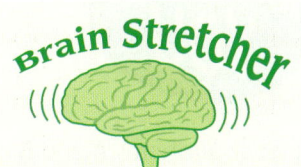

OVER TO YOU

4 Look at painting **A**, which is called *The Angry Christ*. Why do you think the artist has shown Jesus like this?

5 Using the weblinks suggested, go to the CAT website and find out more about their work. What is their prayer for those in prison? Look at their newsletter and read about what has happened in recent campaigns.

6 Why do you think it is important to write to prisoners of conscience?

7 Write a letter to an imaginary person who is unjustly imprisoned.

8 Write two diary entries, one as a prisoner of conscience just after you have been imprisoned, and the other the day you receive a letter from a CAT campaigner.

Brain Stretcher

'Better to light one small candle than to curse the darkness' (Chinese proverb).

What idea is being expressed in this proverb? If you put it into action, what things might you do?

WEBLINKS **You will find links for this topic at** www.nelsonthornes.com/exploringre

Is the world a fair place?

This is about ...

- **Thinking about what is fair and unfair about the world in which you live**
- **Understanding divisions in the world between rich and poor countries**
- **Examining the beliefs and work of Christians in fighting unfairness**

Key questions

- **Is the world a fair place?**
- **How is the world divided?**
- **How should we use the world's resources?**
- **What do religions teach about wealth?**
- **What have people done to help?**
- **What do religions teach about fairness and justice?**

Fantastic Facts

Did you know that 80 per cent of the world's wealth is shared among 20 per cent of the world's population?

KEY WORDS

- Archbishop
- Community
- Fairness
- Freedom
- Injustice
- Justice
- Mass
- Unfairness

1 Look at photos **A** and **B**.

a What do you think their lives are like? Write a short description for each photo.

b How fair is it that one teenager has so many more things than the other? Why might this teenager have so much more? Write down your views.

If you spent time finding out how the world's resources and wealth are shared between the people who live in it, you will discover that there is a huge **unfairness** between the countries. Most northern countries are considered to be rich and well developed. These include the UK, other European countries and North American countries like the USA and Canada. In poorer, less economically developed countries, people live on far less money, there is a lot of unemployment and there are fewer basic public services.

Many countries in South America are very poor, and they have often been controlled by corrupt rulers and brutal dictators. When this happened, the people who lived there suffered great **injustice** and lack of **freedom**. To try to do something about this, some Christians – inspired by the teachings and example of Jesus – stood up against oppression and fought against poverty and lack of human freedom.

Oscar Romero, a Roman Catholic who lived a quiet life of prayer, was one of those who fought for justice. He was **Archbishop** of San Salvador, the capital of El Salvador in South America. At this time, El Salvador was ruled by a corrupt regime and many citizens were suffering. One day, Oscar Romero saw his friend, also a priest, shot dead.

He decided he could not stay silent any longer. He began to preach against the government, organising public demonstrations against the wrongs that were taking place. As a Christian, he was inspired by Jesus's example – Jesus stood up for the poor and for fairness and freedom. Unfortunately, every time Oscar Romero did this, he risked his life, just like Jesus. In 1980 he was shot through the heart while saying **Mass**.

Oscar Romero

Maria Cristina Gomez was a Baptist Christian in San Salvador where she taught Sunday School and worked as a primary school teacher. She dedicated herself to helping people in war-torn El Salvador, where people were poor, many could not read and women were treated badly. She would go into the villages to teach people to read and help them to have a say in how they organised themselves.

On 5 April 1989, as she was leaving school, armed guards dragged Maria away in sight of the children. Her body was later found by the roadside. She had been beaten and shot to death.

The Maria Cristina Gomez Cross

Those who knew Maria and loved her paid for the Maria Cristina Gomez Cross to celebrate her life and her faith lived out in ordinary, everyday aspects of her life – working in the fields, at her home, at school and in the local **community**.

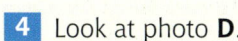

2 Read these passages from the Bible:

a   Psalm 146:7.
b   Luke 3:11.
c   Luke 4:18–19.

Why was it so important to Oscar Romero to help the oppressed in South America?

3 In helping the people of El Salvador, Oscar Romero was breaking the law. Do you think he was right to do this? Give reasons for your opinion.

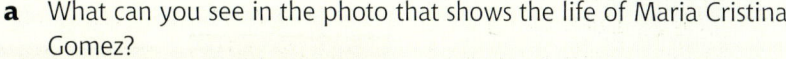

4 Look at photo **D**.

a   What can you see in the photo that shows the life of Maria Cristina Gomez?
b   In the cross, why do you think Maria has her arms raised up?

5 Design a cross to show the life of Oscar Romero.

6 Why do you think people like Oscar Romero and Maria Cristina Gomez continued in their work knowing that it could lead to their death?

7 Imagine you are Oscar Romero or Maria Cristina Gomez. Write a letter to the religious leaders in the UK explaining what has happened to you, the decisions you made and why you made them.

Freedom and justice — *Our journey*

In our journey through this unit, we have:

- discussed the important concepts of freedom and justice

- learned about people, such as Terry Waite and Richard Wurmbrand, who gave up their freedom when they made a stand against injustice

- explored how these concepts have been at the centre of much thought and activity for religious believers

- considered questions such as 'Are we really free?' and explored the idea that some Christians, even when in prison, still claim to be free

- considered how there are always consequences to our actions, a theme that is highlighted in the Hindu idea of karma

- explored the concept of freedom, which is important to Jewish believers, and Pesach is an annual celebration of this

- looked at the stand taken by religious leaders against wrongdoing

Key questions

- What are my views on **justice** and injustice in the world?

- What different kinds of **freedom** are there?

OVER TO YOU

1 a In pairs or small groups, produce concept maps on the themes of 'freedom' and 'justice'. Use your knowledge and understanding of this topic to help you.

b Discuss the links and why you have made them.

c Compare your 'freedom' concept map with the one you produced for task 5 on page 27.

2 What have you learned about your own freedom and **responsibility**? What things, if any, have changed how you think now?

3 What is your view of justice and **injustice** in the world? Do you want to change anything? Explain why.

KEY WORDS

- **Freedom**
- **Injustice**
- **Justice**
- **Pesach**
- **Responsibility**

Help!

Concept maps
A concept map is a group of concepts linked to a topic or theme. You need to work out what you think the links and relationships are. Draw lines between the words and write on them what you think the links are.

A

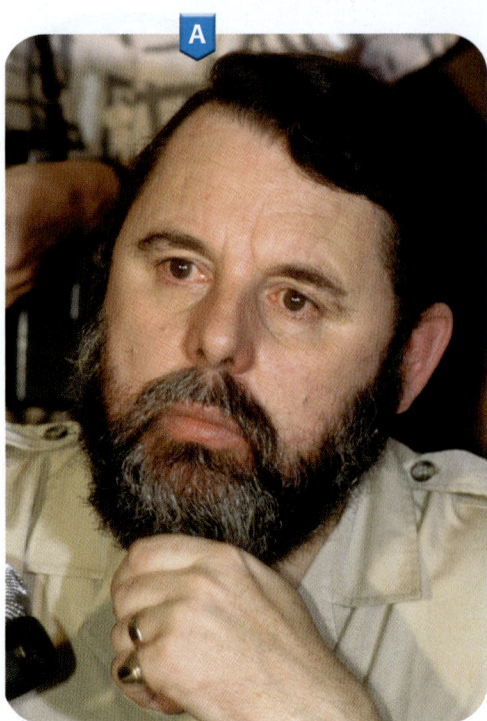

4 Look at photos **A–E**. Complete a large copy of the table below to summarise how each person is linked to the theme of freedom and justice.

Person	What did they say or do about freedom and justice?	What have I learned from this?
Terry Waite		
Jesus		
Martin Luther King		
Anne Frank		
Oscar Romero		

5 Consider carefully the quotes below. What kind of freedom are they referring to?

a 'From the prodigious hilltops of New Hampshire, let freedom ring. From the mighty mountains of New York, let freedom ring. From the heightening Alleghenies of Pennsylvania, let freedom ring … Let freedom ring from every hill and molehill of Mississippi, from every mountainside, let freedom ring!' (Dr Martin Luther King, address at the Lincoln Memorial, 28 August 1963).

b '[Our enemies] may take our lives, but they'll never take our freedom!' (the actor Mel Gibson as William Wallace in the film *Braveheart*).

c 'A man can be free even within prison walls. Freedom is something spiritual. Whoever has once had it can never lose it. There are some people who are never free outside a prison' (Bertold Brecht, German poet and playwright, 1898–1956).

d 'I expect nothing. I fear no one. I am free' (Nikos Kazantzakis, Greek poet and writer, 1883–1957).

e 'My chains fell off, my heart was free/I rose, went forth, and followed Thee' (from a hymn by Charles Wesley, founder of the Methodist Church, 1707–88).

3 Being committed

What is commitment?

This is about ...

- Understanding why people commit themselves to a cause
- Exploring how someone's religious belief gives them courage
- Reflecting on times when you should stand up for what you believe in
- Knowing about special practices linked to religious commitment
- Exploring what it means to belong to a faith community
- Expressing your own views about being committed

Key questions

- Should I speak out for what I believe in?
- Why do people make **sacrifices**?
- Why belong to a **community**?
- Why do people care about others?
- How do religious people show **commitment**?

Which of these sports men and women do you recognise? What do you think they need to do to be committed to their sport?

A

B

C

D

KEY WORDS

- Community
- Commitment
- Rites of passage
- Sacrifice

People are committed to all kinds of things in life and show their commitment by the time and effort they put into it.

For example, athletes and sports stars spend hours in their training so that they can be at the peak of fitness. They need to have physical and mental strength and the necessary skills for their sport.

Some people are committed to their families, their jobs, a cause or a religion. They spend a lot of energy and time on these.

What commitments do you have in your life? Are they to do with your family, friends, pets, etc.?

What do you think these people are committed to?

Some people become committed to a religion and show this commitment in different ways. For example, it might be through a ceremony such as taking bread and wine, or praying five times a day. When someone becomes a member of a faith community, there is often a ritual or celebration that goes along with it. These rituals are often called **rites of passage**.

OVER TO YOU

1 Identify the religions in photos **H–J**. Name the clues you used, for example, clothes.

2 Why do you think people commit themselves to a religion?

3 Make a table of the key celebrations involving commitment from any religions you already know about.

Let's reflect

The French National Assembly has overwhelmingly approved a proposed controversial ban on Muslim headscarves and other 'conspicuous' religious symbols in French schools

If you were committed to Islam and its rules, what would you do?

Should we speak out for our beliefs?

This is about ...

- Considering what you feel strongly about
- Understanding why people show great courage to speak out
- Exploring the story of Pastor Martin Niemoeller
- Expressing your feelings and views about what Pastor Niemoeller did

Key questions

- Should I speak out for what I believe?
- Why should religious people stand up for what they believe?

OVER TO YOU

1. Look at photos **A–C**. Why do you think the people in them have strong feelings?

2. With a partner, list the things you feel really strongly about. What are they? They might be to do with bullying, the price of DVDs, poverty in the world, etc.

3. Discuss any occasions when you have spoken out about something. What was the outcome? Feed this back to the whole class.

When people feel strongly about something, they often demonstrate on the streets.

A

THE PASSION IS A LETHAL WEAPON AGAINST JEWS

B

Socialist Worker
STOP THE WAR
لا للحرب
Contra la guerra
Contro la guerra
Contre la guerre

STOP THE WAR BLAIR MUST GO
Stop the War Coalition
www.stopwar.org.uk

C

EGALITE FRATERNIT

KEY WORDS

- **Chaplain**
- **Communist**
- **Concentration camp**
- **Pastor**
- **Persecution**
- **Socialist**
- **Trade unionist**

> First they came for the **communists**, and I did not speak out –
> because I was not a communist;
> Then they came for the **socialists**, and I did not speak out –
> because I was not a socialist;
> Then they came for the **trade unionists**, and I did not speak out –
> because I was not a trade unionist;
> Then they came for the Jews, and I did not speak out –
> because I was not a Jew;
> Then they came for me –
> and there was no one left to speak out for me.

4 Read the quote in box **D**.

a What kind of person might have said these words?

b When and where might these words been said?

c What do they mean?

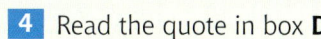
OVER TO YOU

The words in box **D** are by a man called Martin Niemoeller, a Protestant **pastor** who lived in Germany during the Nazi rule. He thought that Hitler was distorting the Christian faith to use it for his own power. He believed the Nazis were breaking God's rules. Niemoeller spoke out against Hitler at a public meeting and the same evening the secret police raided his home. A few days later, a bomb exploded at his home, setting it on fire. Although friends offered to smuggle him and his family to safety, he refused.

Pastor Niemoeller spoke out against the **persecution** of Jews and the Christian Church and was arrested on lots of occasions. Once, while in prison in Berlin, the prison **chaplain** asked him: 'Why are you in prison?' Niemoeller stared back at him and asked: 'Why are you not?'

Niemoeller was imprisoned in Sachsenhausen and Dachau **concentration camps** but managed to survive the war.

Pastor Niemoeller

OVER TO YOU

One of Niemoeller's favourite parts of the Bible was Joshua 1:9: 'Be strong and of good courage: be not frightened, neither be dismayed. For the Lord your God is with you wherever you go.'

5 In groups, discuss:

a Was it easier for Pastor Niemoeller to keep silent or to speak out? Why?

b Why did he choose to speak out?

c Was he right to speak out? Give reasons for your answer.

d What is your view about Pastor Niemoeller?

e How do you feel now about speaking out for something you believe in?

Brain Stretcher

A few days before his death, Niemoeller remarked:

'When I was young I felt I had to carry the gospel. Now that I am old I know that the gospel carries me.'

What do you think he meant?

Inmates in a concentration camp during the Second World War

Why do people make sacrifices?

This is about ...

- Understanding why people commit themselves to a religious way of life
- Exploring why a famous pop star, Cat Stevens, became a Muslim
- Understanding why someone can make such a sacrifice to commit themselves to religion
- Considering how commitment to a religion shows itself in charitable actions

Key questions

- What does it mean to be religious?
- Why do people make sacrifices?

OVER TO YOU

1 How do you feel about each of the following scenarios? Place them on a continuum of 'Gutted' to 'Cool'.

Gutted ————————————————————— Cool

a   You had saved up some money for a CD but you gave it to charity after hearing about the Asian tsunami.
b   You had to visit your grandma with your parents instead of going to youth club.
c   You gave up your seat on a bus to an old man.
d   The friend you were going on holiday with broke his leg – so you stayed at home as well.

Help!

Continuums

A continuum is a line along which you decide to place a word or idea and then discuss your decision with others.

B

A

What do these photos tell you about the same man?

Look at photos **A** and **B**. They are both of Cat Stevens, one of the greatest British pop/folk recording stars. When he was just 19, his first solo album *Matthew and Son* was a hit, after which many of his songs reached the charts in Britain and the USA. He was as well known as the Beatles and the Rolling Stones, and in his short music career he sold more then 40 million records throughout the world.

When he was ill in hospital, Cat Stevens began to think seriously about his life. He did not like what he saw in himself, and so he decided to make a complete break from the past. He was given a copy of the Qur'an and found it contained guidance that explained everything to him.

Cat Stevens took a new name, Yusuf Islam, and became very involved in the local Muslim community, founding one of Britain's top Islamic school chains. He has worked for many charities and his own charity organisation, Small Kindness, is supporting 2,500 orphans in Kosovo and working for Iranian children.

Cat Stevens wrote this about his new experiences:

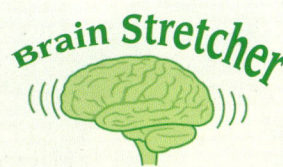

I realised that everything belongs to God … He created everything. At this point I began to lose the pride in me, because hereto I had thought the reason I was here was because of my own greatness. But I realised that I did not create myself, and the whole purpose of my being here was to submit to the teaching that has been perfected by the religion we know as Islam.

Cat Stevens had many hit records

2 Listen to some Cat Stevens songs – you may be able to download them from the Internet.

3 In small groups, discuss the following questions.

 a What do you think are the differences between the lifestyles of Cat Stevens and Yusuf Islam?

 b How difficult may it have been for Cat Stevens to give up fame and fortune to commit himself to a different way of life?

 c What do you think about Cat Stevens's decision to commit himself to Islam and serving others?

Brain Stretcher

In one of his songs, Cat Stevens sang:

'What kind of man can make me turn and see the way I really am?'

Explain what he might have meant by these words.

 **WEBLINKS** **You will find links for this topic at** www.nelsonthornes.com/exploringre

Why do we choose to join communities? (1) Joining the Sikh community

This is about ...

- Understanding why some people want to belong to a religion
- Learning about the Sikh amrit ceremony
- Reflecting on the kinds of commitment shown by Sikhs

Key questions

- Why belong to a community?
- What is it like to join a religious community?

OVER TO YOU

1 Talk with a partner about the communities you see in photos **A–C**.

  a List the responsibilities you might have as a member of each community.

  b Talk about the rules that there might be in each of them.

  c Choose a group that you belong to. Make up a joining ceremony for that group.

KEY WORDS

- Amrit
- Commitment
- Community
- Five Ks
- Guru
- Khalsa
- Punjab

Fantastic Facts

There are 20 million Sikhs worldwide. Britain is home to about half a million Sikhs – the largest number outside the **Punjab**.

A

B

C

Sikhs take part in a welcoming ceremony when they join the Sikh community. The community is called the **Khalsa** and the ceremony is called the **amrit** ceremony. As part of the ceremony, they are reminded of the code of conduct of the Khalsa. This includes wearing the symbol of the Khalsa – the **Five Ks**:

- Kesh (uncut hair) – a symbol of strength and accepting of God's will.
- Kara (a steel bracelet) – reminds the wearer of being devoted to the **Guru**.
- Kanga (a wooden comb) – keeps the hair tidy and represents a clean mind and body.
- Kaccha (cotton shorts) – as symbol of being ready to act for the Guru and of chastity.
- Kirpan (sword) – a sign of the struggle against injustice.

Sikh male members of the Khalsa take the name Singh, which means *lion*, and the Khalsa Sikh women take the name Kaur, which means *princess*.

Kanga

Kesh

The Five Ks

Kara

Kirpan

Kaccha

Recall ...

There is more information about the amrit ceremony on pages 16 –17 of Book 1. You can find out more about the Five Ks and the Khalsa there too.

OVER TO YOU

The ceremony was incredible. Once the doors had been opened, we were led to the main darbar [hall] by the five beloved ones. Everything looked different. It's hard to explain. The best way to describe it is the feeling you get when you've seen something for the first time. I truly felt as if I'd been reborn. From that day forward, I believe that I've lived a better life. I no longer feel alone in times of hardship. I find myself spiritually growing each day, learning and understanding more than I had ever imagined. I knew that taking this step would change my life, but I had no idea how much.

Davinder

If I were asked to briefly describe myself to you, I'd tell you that I'm an average young woman. I have full-length, uncut hair and don't wear makeup. I love listening to rock as well as actively taking part in kirtan [hymns] and I play a Western instrument – the guitar. I'm no different from anyone else and I've made mistakes. The only difference is that I have Guru Ji as my guide. My ardas [prayer] to Guru Ji is to right my wrongs, and teach me how to lead an honest and truthful life.

2 How do you think a young Sikh feels after the amrit ceremony?

3 With a partner, imagine you have recently become a member of the Khalsa. Explain to your partner what life has been like since. What are your responsibilities?

4 With a partner, role play a job interview in which a young Khalsa Sikh is told he must not wear his turban if he gets the job.

5 In small groups, examine the 5Ks. Use the 5Ws model to discuss the subject.

6 What other items do you know that believers have to wear to show that they are members of a faith community?

Help!

5Ws
Discuss **what** it is, **where** and **when** you might see it, **who** might have it and **why**.

Why do we choose to join communities? (2) Joining Christian and Hindu communities

This is about ...

- **Understanding why some people want to belong to a religion**
- **Learning about Christian and Hindu joining ceremonies**
- **Reflecting on the kinds of commitment shown by Christians and Hindus**

Key questions

- **Why belong to a community?**
- **What is it like to join a religious community?**

KEY WORDS

- Baptise
- Bishop
- Cathedral
- Commitment
- Community
- Confirmation
- Guru
- Holy Communion
- Holy Spirit
- Responsibilities
- Samskara

Many people are **baptised** when they are babies. For Christians, this is a joining ceremony to celebrate becoming a member of the local and worldwide Christian **community**. It is sometimes called 'christening'. Because babies cannot make promises, the parents and godparents make promises for them. When those children are older, they can 'confirm' the promises themselves. In the Anglican Church and Roman Catholic Church, they usually do this when they become teenagers, but there is no age limit. **Confirmation** shows that they have decided themselves to make a personal commitment to being a Christian.

A confirmation ceremony

A

Recall ...

What is the difference between infant baptism and believers' baptism?

OVER TO YOU

1 Read Rajvinder's account of her amrit ceremony again on page 47 and compare it with Philip's experiences at his confirmation.

   a What similarities are there in the two ceremonies?

   b What can you find that is different?

2 What do you think is the main difference between infant baptism and the confirmation ceremony in Christianity?

3 What do you think Philip means when he says his commitment to God was 'something personal'?

4 In what ways do you think Philip is more committed after his confirmation? Explain why you think this is.

Philip

*I was christened when I was a child and I didn't think much more about it. But recently I went on an Alpha Course with a friend. It's a kind of a modern teaching course for people who don't know much about Christianity. The Alpha Course made my **commitment** to God something personal rather than something I was brought up to do. That was the first time I thought about it as a personal thing and I feel it even more strongly now.*

B

When the vicar invited people to be confirmed, I jumped at the chance. I had to attend some classes to prepare for it. Two of my friends came along too. The vicar explained that it's like renewing the promises your parents made for you when you were christened.

*The actual ceremony took place at the **cathedral** with the **bishop**. He put his hand on our heads and said a short prayer over each of us. Then he put the sign of the cross on our foreheads with some faintly scented oil. The bishop prayed that the **Holy Spirit** would come upon us with these words: 'Confirm Lord, your servant with your heavenly grace that he may continue yours forever and daily increase in your Holy Spirit more and more until he comes into your everlasting kingdom.' It was a brilliant event and I'm glad my family was there to witness it.*

*The service also included **Holy Communion** – eating bread and drinking wine to remind us of the last meal Jesus ate before he died. When you are confirmed, you are allowed to take part in this for the first time. Since then, I always try to have a 'quiet time' with God every night. My friends at school know I'm a Christian. It's certainly changed my life – I'm much closer to God and I want to serve him in my life.*

In the Hindu community, there is an important ceremony in the life of every boy who belongs to one of the three main castes. The ceremony takes place when the boy is between the ages of seven and twelve, and it marks the beginning of a different kind of life for him. It is the tenth **samskara** (step in life) in Hinduism. This ceremony is more common in Indian Hindu families than in Hindu families in the UK.

The boy prepares for the ritual with his **guru** (religious teacher). His guru presents him with a sacred thread. This is a loop of cotton that the boy wears over his left shoulder and across his body to his right hip. The guru then says a prayer requesting that the boy continues to grow in faith. The sacred thread must be worn at all times and when it wears out the boy will buy a new one. He is now a full member of his caste and must accept all the **responsibilities** that go with it.

These responsibilities are:

- to worship God
- to respect the holy men and holy writings
- to respect his elders, including his parents
- to help the poor
- to care for animals and all living things.

C

The sacred thread ceremony

OVER TO YOU

5 a Think about the three different joining ceremonies you have read about. What things do they have in common?

b Draw a Venn diagram to show what these ceremonies have in common and what differences there are.

6 Draw a simple timeline of someone's life. Decide on four special times. Where do the joining ceremonies you have read about come on your timeline?

Help!

Venn diagrams

Venn diagrams show what things have in common, and what the differences are.

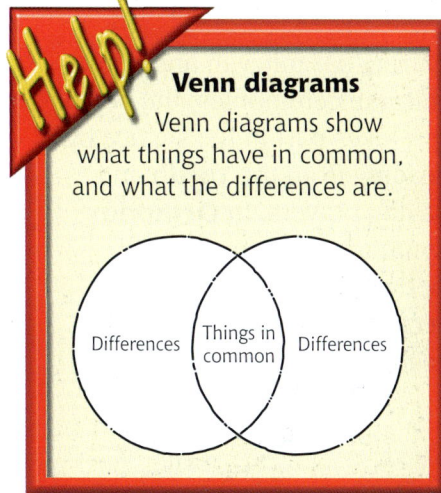

Differences | Things in common | Differences

WEBLINKS **You will find links for this topic at** www.nelsonthornes.com/exploringre

When am I grown up?

This is about ...

- **Considering what is involved in growing up**
- **Understanding the importance of bar mitvah and bat mitzvah for Jews**
- **Listening to the views of a Jewish boy talking about his bar mitzvah**

Key questions

- What responsibilities will I have when I am grown up?
- What does it feel like to belong to a religious community?
- What responsibilities do religious people have when they join their faith community?

Young Jewish people have a coming of age and **commitment** ceremony called **bar mitzvah** (for boys on their thirteenth birthday) and **bat mitzvah** (for girls on their twelfth birthday). The words mean 'son of the commandment' and 'daughter of the commandment'.

The ceremonies mark the time when a young person is recognised as an adult in the Jewish **community** and now has to follow the rules of Jewish life for themselves. Both rituals are held in the **synagogue** on **Shabbat**, and are followed by a party to celebrate. Family, friends and members of the synagogue come to celebrate the young person's coming of age.

During bar mitzvah and bat mitzvah ceremonies, the boy or girl takes part in the service by reading from the **Torah** and saying prayers. In **Orthodox** synagogues, the girl reads perhaps from the psalms or recites some poetry instead of reading from the Torah.

A

C

B

1 Look at photos **A–C** and, in pairs, discuss at what age you can do these things. At what age do you think they should take place?

KEY WORDS

- **Bar mitzvah**
- **Bat mitzvah**
- **Commitment**
- **Community**
- **Orthodox**
- **Responsibilities**
- **Shabbat**
- **Synagogue**
- **Tallit**
- **Tefillin**
- **Torah**

Children prepare for their bar/bat mitzvah by going to the synagogue religious school some years before to learn about Jewish customs and the Hebrew language. They also learn how to read the Torah, pray and use the **tallit** (prayer shawl) and **tefillin** (phylacteries).

OVER TO YOU

2 Find out more information about the tallit and the tefillin.

3 Produce a timeline of the events leading up to and including a bar mitzvah.

4 Imagine you have just had your bar/bat mitzvah. In what way do you now feel different? Complete a fortune line of the events involved. You could include some of the following: learning Hebrew; reading from the Torah or psalms; having a party; being regarded as an adult; helping out at a religion school.

My dad wants me to have my bar mitzvah in Israel, but I want it at Old Trafford.

5 Imagine a younger brother is coming up to his bar mitzvah. Write to him telling him all he needs to do to prepare.

Today is my big day – it's the day of my bar mitzvah. To prepare, I have been going to my religion school since the age of seven and have had to practise my Hebrew and go to the synagogue regularly. I will be reading a section from the Torah, which are the Five Books of Moses, and I will also be reading the Readings of the Prophets in Hebrew.

Before I recite all the Hebrew, I will have to explain what I am reading to the congregation in English. Reading from the scrolls is more difficult than reading normal Hebrew because all the vowels are taken out of the words and it's all handwritten on parchment.

What does my bar mitzvah mean to me? It means I will be treated more like an adult within my community. I can also help out at our religion school, which means I am paying back for what I have been taught and teaching the younger generation. It means I can take part in more services. And I get presents to mark this important moment in my life. After my bar mitzvah, I am going to help out at our religion school. My bar mitzvah has made me more confident with my Hebrew and speaking in front of a lot of people.

Nathaniel

6 a Produce an invitation inviting people to a bar mitzvah.

b Plan a bar mitzvah party.

7 a What responsibilities do Jewish young people have after their bar or bat mitzvah?

b What responsibilities will you have when you are grown up?

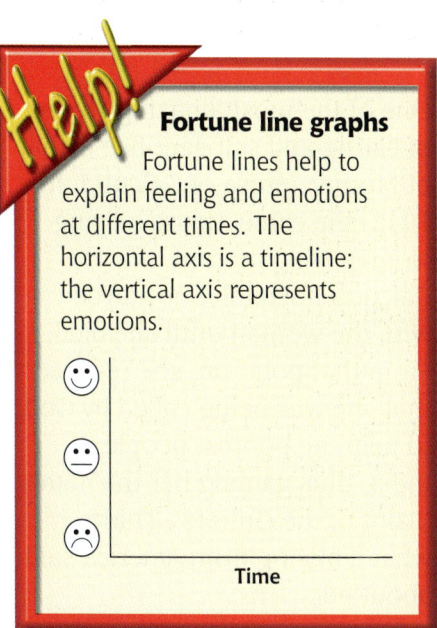

Help!

Fortune line graphs

Fortune lines help to explain feeling and emotions at different times. The horizontal axis is a timeline; the vertical axis represents emotions.

Time

Why do people care about others?

This is about ...

- **Considering why people care about others**
- **Learning about the work of Mother Teresa**
- **Understanding how being a Christian involves caring and sacrifice**

OVER TO YOU

1. Look at photos **A–C** of people caring for others. What do you think their care involves? In what ways might they be making **sacrifices**?

2. In small groups, brainstorm other ways in which people care for others. What kinds of sacrifices might they be making?

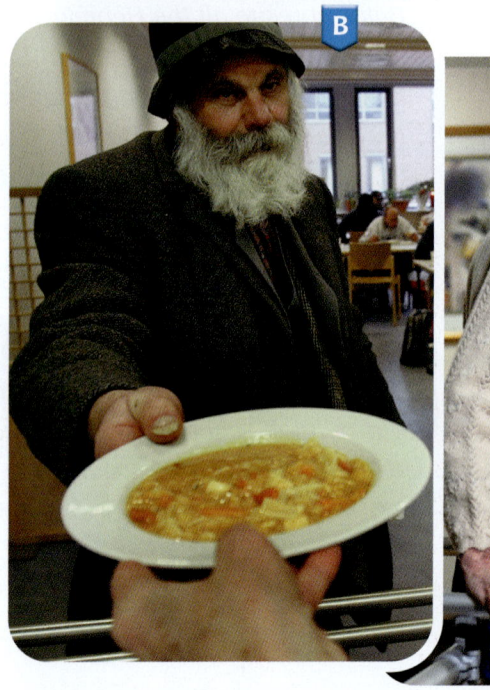

Key questions

- **What work did Mother Teresa do?**
- **How does being a Christian involve sacrifice?**

KEY WORDS

- **Commitment**
- **Evangelism**
- **Sacrifice**

One of the most amazing stories of caring and self-sacrifice is that of Mother Teresa of Calcutta. In 1948, she came across a dying woman lying in front of a Calcutta hospital. She stayed with the woman until she died. From that point on, she realised that she was being called by God to help the poorest people in India, thus gaining her the name 'Saint of the Gutters'. This is what a bishop from America said about her.

Mother Teresa imitated Christ and her life was a lesson in love. As she personally tended the sick and the dying in Calcutta's slums, she helped people there and beyond see the material and spiritual poverty that confronts modern society.

As small and soft-spoken as she was, her reach was large and her message heard around the world. She saw Jesus in everyone – from the child in the womb, to the sick and vulnerable, especially those afflicted with Aids, to the aged and dying abandoned in the streets of Calcutta. She urged people everywhere to reach beyond themselves to heal those hurting about them.

3 Mother Teresa talked about the dying, the unloved and the unwanted as being 'Jesus in disguise'.

   a Read the parable of the sheep and the goats in the Bible. You can find it in Matthew 25.

   b Jesus says in this parable: 'Whatever you did for these brothers of mine, you did for me.' What do you think this means?

   c What is the link between Mother Teresa's words and Jesus's parable?

4 Write a magazine article on the life of Mother Teresa with the title 'Angel of Mercy'. You need to research her life and the organisation she started for this.

Mother Teresa

D

Not everyone can make the sorts of sacrifices Mother Teresa made for the sick and vulnerable people she cared for. However, millions of people around the world do make a **commitment** to caring for others. One way is being involved in a charity – either working for an organisation or giving money to help its work.

Smile International is a Christian charity. Its spokesperson says: 'Our aim is to share the love of Jesus through **evangelism** and aid distribution and by so doing put a smile on people's faces as they see the love of God in action.'

The people who work for Smile offer practical support and encouragement to poor and needy people around the world whose lives are affected by war, poverty and illness. They are currently working in countries such as Albania, Kosovo, Macedonia, Montenegro and Bulgaria.

The shoebox appeal is an example of one of Smile's projects. It sends shoeboxes full of useful presents to families, villages, schools and camps in Eastern European countries.

You could send a shoebox to help someone your own age, a younger child or a family. Think about what things they might like. These sorts of items are popular:

- Toiletries: toothbrushes, toothpaste, flannels, soap.
- Writing materials: notebooks, drawing pads, pens, pencils.
- Clothes: hats, scarves, gloves, socks.
- Small toys: dolls, cars, balls, cuddly toys, skipping ropes.

Cover the lid and box separately with colourful wrapping paper and put the presents inside. Put the lid on the box and secure it with a strong elastic band. More details, together with information on where to send your shoebox, can be found on the Exploring RE website.

 **You will find links for this topic at**
www.nelsonthornes.com/exploringre

Brain Stretcher

'It is not how much we do, but how much love we put in the doing. It is not how much we give, but how much love we put in the giving.'

What did Mother Teresa mean when she said these words?

Let's reflect

'When a poor person dies of hunger, it has not happened because God did not take care of him or her. It has happened because neither you nor I wanted to give that person what he or she needed' (Mother Teresa, 1910–97).

What do you think of Mother Teresa's words? If you agree with them, explain why.

Why do some Christians have bread and wine?

This is about ...

- **Exploring the meaning of symbols**
- **Understanding the symbolism of bread and wine in Christian worship**
- **Knowing that some Christians take bread and wine to show that they are committed to Christianity**
- **Reflecting on what Christians might feel as they take part in the service**

Key questions

- **What is Holy Communion?**
- **What symbols are important to Christians?**

Receiving Holy Communion

A

KEY WORDS

- **Breaking of Bread**
- **Commitment**
- **Eucharist**
- **Holy Communion**
- **Holy Liturgy**
- **Lord's Supper**
- **Mass**
- **Resurrection**
- **Symbol**

B

These signs are used in different countries across the world. Can you work out what they mean?

A **symbol** is something that represents or stands for something else. Road signs, like the ones in picture **B**, include symbols. They can be used all over the world because everyone understands what they represent without needing any extra information.

Some symbols have several meanings, a hidden meaning or a deeper meaning. Religions often have symbols like these. Religions deal with important, difficult questions and symbols can help believers understand complicated religious messages. They can also be a badge of membership, a sign of **commitment**.

The Bible says that Jesus knew he was going to be killed. The night before Jesus was arrested, he had a meal with his disciples (followers). There was bread and wine at the meal. Jesus broke up the bread and gave a piece to each of his disciples. He told them the bread was his body. Each disciple ate a piece. Then Jesus poured wine into a cup and told them it was his blood. The cup was passed around for everyone to drink from.

The bread and wine

Fantastic Facts

Christianity first started as a religion at the time of the Roman Empire. The Roman authorities persecuted Christians because they would not worship the Roman Emperor as a god. The authorities spread rumours that Christians were cannibals, saying they ate human bodies in their worship.

Today, many Christians have bread and wine in their church services to remember Jesus's sacrifice. The bread stands for the body of Jesus and the wine for his blood. Christians believe that in his death and **resurrection**, Jesus forgave the sins of people. The Christian message is that Jesus made the ultimate sacrifice for all humans and his body was broken and his blood was spilled in order to do this.

The meal of bread and wine is an important act for Christians because they talk about Jesus being with them at the service through the symbols of the bread and wine. Therefore, they see it as a celebration. They are giving thanks for the death of Jesus, which gave them salvation.

The taking of bread and wine in church has all sorts of names in different types of Christianity – **Holy Communion**; the **Eucharist** (from a Greek word meaning 'thanksgiving'); the **Lord's Supper**; the **Mass**; the **Breaking of Bread**; the **Holy Liturgy**. For many Christians, it is the most important part of worship in church and a powerful way of showing their commitment to following Jesus Christ.

OVER TO YOU

1 The Christian message is that Jesus died to save all people from sin. What does 'sin' mean? Write down five things you think are sins.

2 Imagine you are a Christian believer who takes bread and wine in your church service. Write a letter explaining this practice to a friend who never goes to church.

3 Spend some time looking at painting **D**. It is called *Last Supper* and is by an artist called Judith Wolfe.

   a What are your feelings when you look at this painting?

   b What does it say about the use of bread and wine?

Last Supper

Faith CONNECTIONS

Examine some other religious ceremonies that show people's commitment to their faith.

These might include prayer times in Islam or the arti ceremony in Hinduism.

Brain Stretcher

Read the story of the last supper in the Bible, Matthew 26:26–30. What do you think it means when Jesus says: 'This is my blood, which seals God's covenant'?

In our journey through this unit, we have:

- discussed courage and commitment

- met religious people who have stood up for their beliefs or showed great commitment and sacrifice

- learned about ceremonies and rituals linked to religious commitment

- heard from young religious people what belonging to a faith community means

- reflected on what our views are about such commitment

Key questions

- What am I committed to?

- How do people show **commitment** to their religion?

KEY WORDS

- Commitment
- Community
- Sacrifice

OVER TO YOU

1 We know that commitment to people sometimes goes wrong. Think about David and Victoria Beckham. What is the story of their commitment? Are they still committed to each other?

2 How committed are you? What do you find important enough to spend time and energy doing? Do you think it is important to be committed?

  a In pairs, choose three things you are committed to.
  b Show on the commitment ladder where you are in relation to each one.
  c Give your reasons for being where you are.
  d Do you want to get up the ladder? If so, what is stopping you? How can you climb higher on your commitment ladder?.

Help!

Commitment ladders

Commitment ladders can be used to show how committed you are to something. The higher up the ladder you go, the more committed you feel.

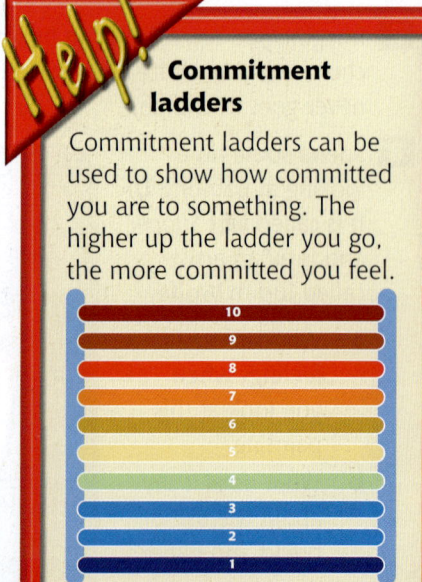

You need to *see* commitment. People who are part of a faith **community** usually show this in some way. It might be through what they wear, what they eat, what they say, what they do and where they go.

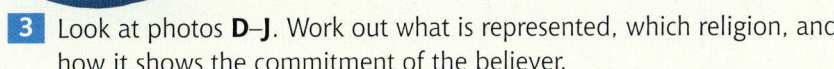
OVER TO YOU

3 Look at photos **D–J**. Work out what is represented, which religion, and how it shows the commitment of the believer.

Use a large copy of the table below. The first example has been completed to help you.

Photo	What is represented?	Which religion?	How does it show the believer's commitment?
D	Hijab	Islam	Worn to tell others they are a Muslim
E			

D

F

E

G

H

I

J

This is about ...

- **Considering why there is so much violence today**
- **Understanding religious views on violence**
- **Appreciating the variety of viewpoints within religions**
- **Exploring how violence and war can result from religious differences**
- **Knowing about religious groups and communities that can have a healing influence**
- **Reflecting on how it is possible to live peacefully**

Key questions

- **What makes someone violent?**
- **What causes conflict?**
- **What is peace?**
- **Is it ever right to go to war?**
- **Why does religion sometimes cause wars?**
- **How can religion bring healing?**
- **Should religious people go to war?**

OVER TO YOU

A

B

C

KEY WORDS

- Community
- Conflict
- Peace

D

Schoolboy was 'stabbed in heart'

The final movements of a schoolboy who was fatally stabbed outside a classroom have been shown on CCTV at the trial of a teenager accused of killing him.

Luke Walmsley, 14, was knifed through the heart at Birkbeck Secondary School in North Somercotes, Lincolnshire, in November 2003.

His parents watched tearfully as Nottingham Crown Court was shown footage of him with a bloody chest.

A 16-year-old boy, who cannot be named, has denied a charge of murdering Luke.

From the BBC News website (news.bbc.co.uk), 8 July 2004

1. Look at pictures **A–C** and read the newpaper article in box **D**.
   - **a** What are your feelings as you study these images?
   - **b** What other kinds of violence can you think of?
2. What do you think causes violence? Carry out a survey of your classmates. Give them the following possibilities and ask them to suggest any additional ones.
   - **a** Computer games.
   - **b** Television programmes.
   - **c** Films.
   - **d** Religion.
   - **e** Alcohol.
   - **f** Physical abuse.
   - **g** Music.
3. In small groups, explore some examples and discuss how these cause violence.

In this unit we will be looking at how conflict and violence in our society and throughout the world cause so many problems. People from different faith **communities** have formed views about this topic and we will see that they do not always agree with each other. All religions condemn war but many believers will take part in it under some circumstances.

There are lots of possible triggers for violence and we will probably act in different ways according to what the situation is and what we believe. In order to think about our views, and before we look at some of these issues in more depth in this unit, try exploring your own views and feelings.

I've been brought up in a Christian home and I suppose most of what I believe is Christian. When Jesus said 'Love your neighbour', I can live with that. But when he said 'If someone strikes you on the right cheek, turn the other one' I can't go along with that. Surely God doesn't expect me to roll over and let people do what they want to me.

Ben

OVER TO YOU

4 In pairs, discuss the following scenarios.
How would you react to them? Would you use violence? Rate them on a scale of possible violent response using the traffic light technique.

   a A man breaks into your house and threatens your family with a knife. You have easy access to a shotgun.

   b You are shopping when a man enters the store holding a gun, saying he will shoot anyone who moves. He stands with his back to you.

   c Someone deliberately bumps into you in the street and laughs.

   d You have just bought a new car. In the night, the alarm goes off and when you look outside you can see someone trying to break into it.

   e You are 18 years old. Your country has been invaded by a neighbouring country. There is an appeal for all those over 18 to join the armed forces.

   f You are in the air force, fighting in a war. Your mission is to drop a nuclear bomb on an enemy country.

5 a Some religious people have taken a completely non-violent approach to life based on the teachings of their sacred books. However, Charlie does not think he can do this. Read what he says, then discuss with a partner what your reaction is to his comments? Do you agree or not? Explain your views.

   b List some occasions when you think using violence would be necessary.

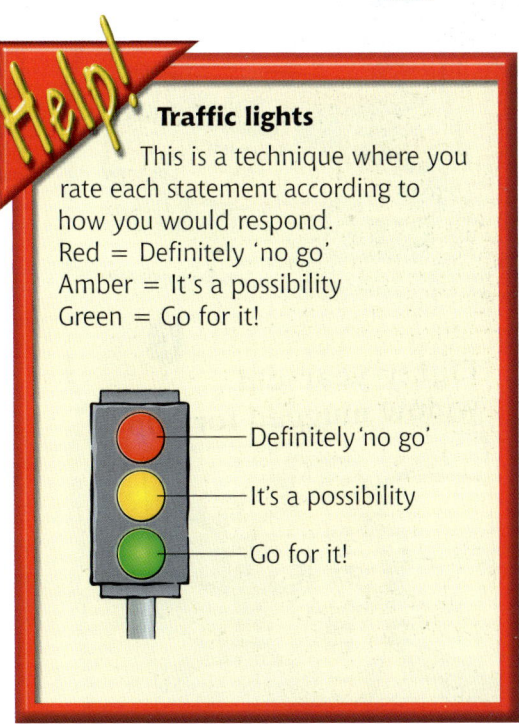

Help!

Traffic lights

This is a technique where you rate each statement according to how you would respond.
Red = Definitely 'no go'
Amber = It's a possibility
Green = Go for it!

Definitely 'no go'

It's a possibility

Go for it!

Should I always forgive?

This is about ...

- **Exploring what it means to forgive**
- **Understanding how Christians can forgive in tragic circumstances**
- **Knowing about the significance of Rosh Hashanah for Jews**
- **Reflecting on the importance of forgiveness**

Key questions

- **How important is it to forgive?**
- **What does religion teach about forgiveness?**

A Mass murderer caught after 15th victim

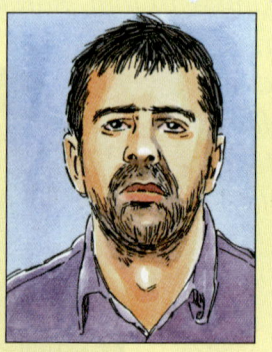

B Joyriders wreck kids' trip abroad

COMMUNITY MINIBUS

C Eighty-year-old widow mugged for 50p

OVER TO YOU

1 In pairs, make up a short story with the title 'I'll never forgive you for that!'

2 With the same partner, look at newspaper headlines **A**–**C**. They are all about situations where it may be hard for people to forgive. Rate each one on a sliding scale of 1 to 5.

Help!

Sliding scales

This activity means using a scale of numbers from 1 to 5 to rank your response. 1 = Very hard to forgive and 5 = Very easy to forgive.

Help!

Mind maps

A mind map starts with a main idea or topic in the middle of the page, with branches to sub-topics that branch our further again. Use drawings and colours to make your mind maps clear, as well as writing the links along the branches.

OVER TO YOU

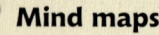

3 In pairs, look again at the newspaper headlines and discuss what you can see.
   a Who might be involved in each story (for example, victim, family)?
   b Who do you think may find it hardest to forgive the people who have done wrong? Explain why.

4 a Make a list of ten everyday occasions when people do things that need to be forgiven, for example, saying something hurtful.
   b Discuss what would be the results if:
   i   they were forgiven
   ii they were not forgiven.
   What do you think brings about the best outcome?

5 Produce a mind map based on the theme of 'forgiveness'.

Just before 11.00 am on 8 November 1987, a bomb exploded without warning as people gathered at the war memorial in Enniskillen, Northern Ireland, for the annual Remembrance Day service. Eleven people were killed and sixty-three injured. The **IRA** admitted responsibility the following day and expressed 'deep regret'. Gordon Wilson and his daughter Marie were trapped in the rubble. Marie later died, but her father survived. Mr Wilson was later interviewed and he shocked many people by saying that, as a Christian, he forgave the terrorists who had killed his daughter and would pray for them. He also said he did not want anyone to take revenge for the bombing. Some people supported his views, but others criticised him.

People send cards to each other at Rosh Hashanah

The Jewish festival of **Rosh Hashanah** is both a fun time and a serious occasion. It is a fun time because it is the Jewish New Year and a celebration of God's creation of human beings. Families come together for the holiday meal. They eat apples and bread dipped in honey in the hope of blessings and sweetness in the year ahead.

It is also a serious time as people take seriously the need to say sorry, forgive others and put themselves right with God. It marks the time when Jews give their apologies for any hurt they may have caused others and any wrongs they have done. Ten days after Rosh Hashanah comes **Yom Kippur**, the Day of **Atonement**. This is the day when Jews confess to God what they have done wrong, saying sorry and asking for forgiveness.

The **shofar** is one of the earliest Jewish instruments. It is usually made from a ram's horn and was used in biblical times to announce an important event, such as the approach of an army or an oncoming disaster, or to call everyone together. The shofar is blown on Rosh Hashanah and at the end of Yom Kippur to signal the new year with its new beginnings.

Blowing the shofar

OVER TO YOU

6 Imagine you have just heard Gordon Wilson's interview. What would you say to him if you met him?

7 Why are Christians expected to forgive? Research the following Bible passages to come to a conclusion:

  a Jesus was asked by Peter, 'How many times shall I forgive my brother?' (Matthew 18:21).

  b Jesus told a parable about the unforgiving servant (Matthew 18:21–35).

  c Jesus told the well-known parable of the forgiving father (Luke 15:11–32).

8 **a** In small groups, think back to some recent news stories and make a list of some bad things that have happened.

  b Decide who needs to ask forgiveness from whom and how the situation could be resolved.

OVER TO YOU

9 Your teacher will play some quiet music. Meditate on the shofar and think of any things you have said or done for which you should apologise.

10 Design and produce a Jewish New Year card. What symbols will you use? Explain why.

 **Help!**

Stilling and meditation

Stilling is simply to be still and relaxed and meditation is to concentrate on something to help you think more deeply.

Let's reflect

About 3,600 people were killed in **conflict** in Northern Ireland between 1966 and 1999.

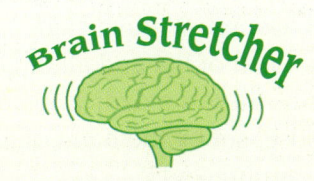

Brain Stretcher

'Love is an act of endless forgiveness' (Peter Ustinov, English actor and author, 1921–2004).

What do you think this quote means?

Does religion cause wars?

This is about ...

- **Knowing about examples of religious conflict**
- **Understanding why religious people sometimes find themselves divided**
- **Considering what is involved in working for peace**

Key questions

- Why do religious people find themselves in **conflict**?
- How can people work towards **peace** in society?

KEY WORDS

- **Community**
- **Conflict**
- **Peace**

You may have heard people say that although religions talk about love, it is religion that causes most wars. Do you believe this is the case? It is true that while religion can bring people together, it can also force them apart.

At a prayer meeting shortly before the invasion of Iraq in 2003, George W Bush said, 'Behind all of life and all of history, there's a dedication and purpose, set by the hand of a just and faithful God.'

But in Baghdad, Saddam Hussein told Iraqis, 'Fight as God ordered you to do.' Osama bin Laden also regards the campaign being waged by his terror network as a religious duty.

Who are these men? What do they have to do with recent wars?

OVER TO YOU

1 Below are some examples of conflict that involve religion in some way or another. Try to match them up. Talk about what you know of them.

The Crusades	Ayatollah Khomeini calling for his death
Mahatma Gandhi	Catholics and Protestants clashing
The Holocaust	Muslims and Croats fighting
Northern Ireland	Christians and Muslims fighting
Salman Rushdie	Assassinated by a militant Hindu
Mostar Bridge, Croatia	More than six million Jews killed

Why do you think this is called a peace wall?

I visited Belfast recently with some friends. We stayed at the Europa Hotel, which is described in the tourist information leaflets as the most bombed hotel in Europe. That sounded really scary. We had learned about the 'troubles' in Northern Ireland in our history lessons. What was happening now?

We took one of the famous black taxi tours to see the sights of Belfast. What I found amazing was that there are still Catholic and Protestant areas. The Catholic Falls area is divided from the Protestant Shankill area by a 'peace line' – a large wall. In the Protestant **community***, which supports the British government, we saw pavements painted red, white and blue and there were lots of Union Jacks and other loyalist flags.*

In both areas there are murals of political events or people who have died in the conflict. In Protestant areas, there were murals of hooded gunmen. In Catholic areas, there were military images. We saw a famous one of Bobby Sands, who died during a hunger strike.

Steph

Fantastic Facts

There are hundreds of murals painted on the sides of houses in Belfast. They often represent military figures, political events or people who have died in the conflict.

WEBLINKS **You will find links for this topic at** www.nelsonthornes.com/exploringre

OVER TO YOU

2 In Belfast, the wall has divided two religious communities. What do you think they could do to understand one another better? What steps could they take to improve their relationships?

3 What other religious divisions do you know of today?

4 In pairs, discuss the following questions.

  a Which 'walls' divide people today?

  b Which 'walls' divide religions today?

  c Why might some religious groups turn to fighting?

  d If you were building an imaginary wall of peace between two religious communities, what would it be made of? Think about things such as respect, love, etc.

5 Create a peace wall in your classroom. On each brick, come up with a word, photo, drawing or quote to promote peace.

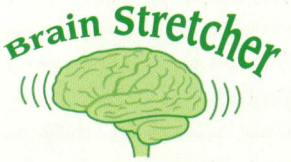

Brain Stretcher

'The future is not a gift: it is an achievement. Every generation helps make its own future. This is the essential challenge of the present' (Robert F Kennedy, US senator, 1925–68).

How do you think this quote relates to what you have been discussing in this topic?

How can religion build bridges?

This is about ...

- **Knowing about an example of religious conflict**
- **Understanding why religious people sometimes find themselves divided**
- **Considering how people, including those with strong religious beliefs, can deal with their differences**

Key questions

- **Why do religious people find themselves in conflict?**
- **How can people work towards peace in society?**

KEY WORDS

- Community
- Conflict
- Guru
- Guru Gobind Singh
- Peace
- Volunteers

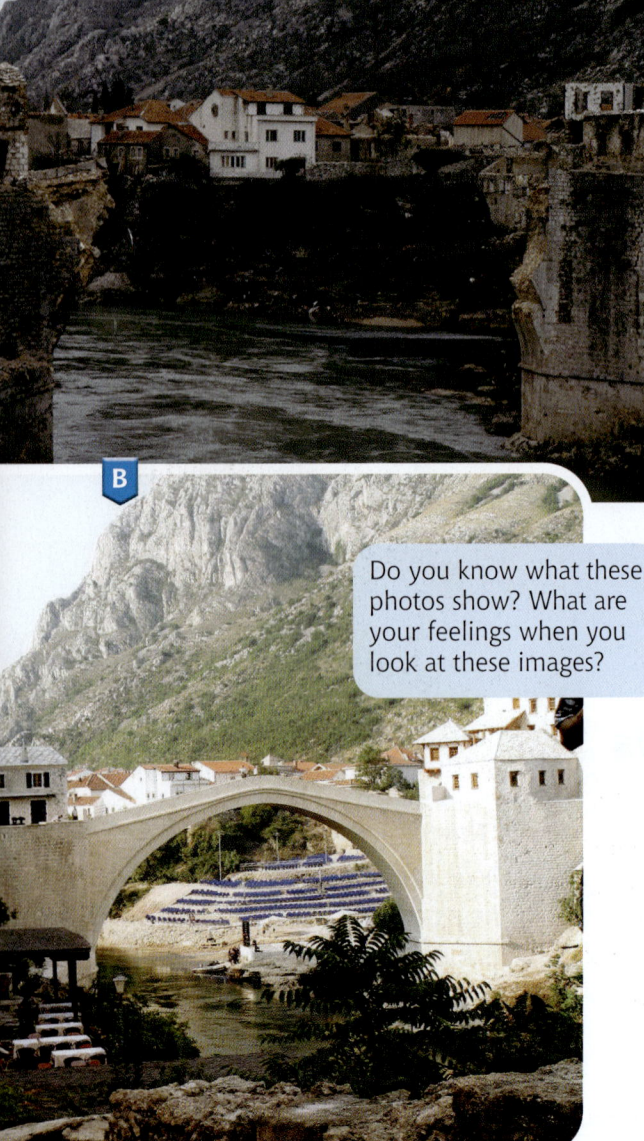

Do you know what these photos show? What are your feelings when you look at these images?

I went with my parents on holiday to Croatia a few years ago. What I didn't expect was a drive through part of Bosnia. I had heard about the war in the old Yugoslavia but it hadn't hit home. It did then as we saw on the sides of the road lots of burned-out houses. We drove into Mostar where there had been a lot of fighting. The beautiful old bridge, the pride of Mostar, which was built over the Neretva River, had been destroyed when Muslims and Bosnian Croats fought from their sides of the town.

My mum explained that, until the war, Mostar was a mixed city of Muslims, Croats (Roman Catholic Christians) and Serbs (Serbian Orthodox Christians). Then it was split into two: Muslims on the east, Croats on the west. Croat artillery took two days to knock the old bridge down.

Last year I saw something on television about the opening of the newly repaired bridge. Hopefully, the new bridge will bring the Muslim and Bosnian Croat sides of Mostar together again, and it will also bring an end to their differences.

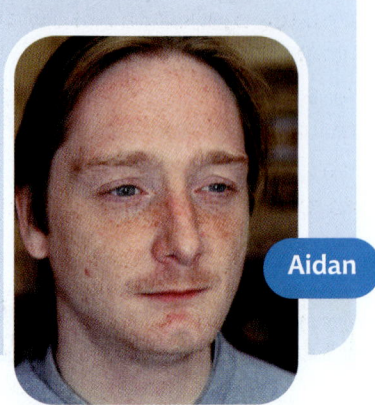

Aidan

OVER TO YOU

1 Using the weblinks suggested, find out more about the city of Mostar.

2 What do you think both sides could do to understand one another more? How do you think they might get on better?

3 In Mostar, people are rebuilding the education system. What do you think they could do or teach in schools to help improve trust and understanding?

4 **a** In small groups, design and build a model of a bridge.

   b After you have finished, consider what skills you used to do this.

5 **a** In Mostar, the river divided two religious communities. Discuss what different 'sides' there are in society today, which need a bridge to bring them together.

   b What name could you give this bridge to sum up what is required to bring the sides together?

6 Your teacher will play some quiet music. Meditate on the bridge you have made or on picture **B** of the Mostar bridge. Think about how people can build bridges to make relationships better. After the meditation, you might want to share your thoughts with others in the class.

OVER TO YOU

7 What are your feelings about the actions of Bhai Kanaya? Would you have complained about him or supported him?

8 Write a letter to the *Sikh Times* expressing your views about Bhai Kanaya.

> To the Sikh Times
>
> Dear Sir/Madam
>
> Re: Bhai Kanaya helps the enemy!

9 Using the weblinks suggested, find out more about the work of Khalsa Aid.

The army of **Guru Gobind Singh** had been fighting against the troops of the Emperor Aurangzeb for a long time. The Sikh fortress was surrounded and many had been wounded and killed on both sides.

A man could be seen in the distance wending his way through the wounded and the dying, carrying water. When he came across someone still alive, he would bend down and give them some water. He was a Sikh called Bhai Kanaya. However, the Sikh soldiers noticed that he was also giving water to the soldiers of the enemy. They complained about this to the **Guru**.

The Guru sent for Bhai Kanaya and asked him whether this was true. Bhai Kanaya explained that when he walked through the battlefield he saw only the wounded, and it was the least he could do to help them, whether friend or enemy.

The Guru was pleased and gave Bhai Khanaya some ointment that could be used on the wounded. Then he would be acting as a true Sikh.

Inspired by the story of Bhai Kanaya, a group of young Sikh **volunteers** in 1999 took time out from their professions and family life and, with the help of the local **community**, put together a convoy of trucks full of relief aid and food and travelled to Kosovo. As a result of this, Khalsa Aid was born. Sikh communities across the world have given money and encouragement to the volunteers to provide relief in emergencies.

C

Khalsa Aid in action

Help!

Stilling and meditation

Stilling is simply to be still and relaxed and meditation is to concentrate on something to help you think more deeply.

WEBLINKS You will find links for this topic at www.nelsonthornes.com/exploringre

How can religion bring peace?

This is about ...

- **Knowing about two religious communities that work to bring peace between people and communities**
- **Understanding how important forgiveness and reconciliation are in religions**
- **Developing skills of empathy and conflict resolution**

Key question

- **How can religion help people to be more peaceful?**

KEY WORDS

- Community
- Conflict
- Empathy
- Peace
- Reconciliation

In 1964, a new Christian **community** called Corrymeela was formed in Northern Ireland to show that people of different traditions can work together, learn about and respect one another, support the victims of violence and bring healing where there is pain and **conflict**.

This community wished to give opportunities for young people, teachers, youth workers and others to meet and build new relationships and trust where once they had been divided. They wanted to discuss how 'enemies' could become 'friends'.

This is how someone who attended a residential weekend described what happened: 'There was a really warm welcome from the staff and members. They gave us space and time to reflect, to listen to one another and share stories from the lives of people who had suffered from violence and conflict.'

A

CORRYMEELA IS PEOPLE OF ALL AGES AND CHRISTIAN TRADITIONS. WHO, INDIVIDUALLY AND TOGETHER ARE COMMITTED TO THE HEALING OF SOCIAL, RELIGIOUS & POLITICAL DIVISIONS THAT EXIST IN NORTHERN IRELAND AND THROUGHOUT THE WORLD

The Corrymeela community

OVER TO YOU

1. What kind of things come into your mind when you think of peace? With a partner, draw a mind map exploring the concept of peace.

2. Using the weblinks suggested, find out more about the Corrymeela community.

3. Write an article for your local newspaper about spending a weekend with the Corrymeela community.

Fantastic Facts

Another group in Belfast, the Cornerstone Community, meets for prayer in a house that actually lies across the peace wall separating Catholic and Protestant areas. It is possible to go through one door from one side and out another door to the other side.

Help!

Mind map

A mind map starts with a main idea or topic at the centre of a page with branches to sub topics which branch out further again. Use drawings and colours as well as writing the connections along the branches.

The city of Coventry is famous for its cathedral. In the Second World War, the city was bombed many times because it had lots of weapons factories. It was the air raid on the night of 14 November 1940 that destroyed the cathedral and killed 568 people. In photo **B** you can see the empty shell of the old cathedral, which still stands today next to the wonderful new cathedral.

Coventry Cathedral after the bombing

New Coventry Cathedral

A day after the bombs, workers found in the rubble that two of the huge rafter beams had fallen across each other, forming the shape of a cross. These were tied together and placed on the ruined altar. Also found among the rubble were three huge rafter nails. One of the clergy bound these together with wire to form another cross, which now hangs in the new cathedral. This cross has become a symbol of a worldwide society of reconciliation known as the Cross of Nails community.

On 13 February 1945, the city of Dresden in Germany was fire-bombed by the RAF and the US Air Force. The city, including the cathedral, was destroyed and 35,000 civilians died. After the war, a group of young people from Dresden came to Coventry to help rebuild the cathedral, and some went to Dresden from Coventry to help rebuild there.

Over the years, the Cross of Nails has become a powerful symbol of **peace** and **reconciliation**. The community organises conferences, works for peace throughout the world and encourages people to be disciplined in their lives with times of silence, prayer and meditation.

The Cross of Nails at Coventry Cathedral

OVER TO **YOU**

5 Using the weblinks suggested, find out more about the Cross of Nails community.

6 The man who made the cross of nails could have made a weapon of nails. What do you think may have been the result if he had done this instead?

7 Why would the Christian community at Coventry want to work for reconciliation? Use these passages from the Bible to help you:

   a   Matthew 5:43–45.
   b   Matthew 6:14–15.
   c   Luke 15:3–7.

8 Role play a conversation between two people, one from Coventry and one from Dresden, whose parents died in the bombings. How could you come to a peaceful conclusion?

WEBLINKS **You will find links for this topic at**
www.nelsonthornes.com/exploringre

Why do we remember 11 September 2001?

This is about ...

- **Understanding reactions to 11 September**
- **Exploring your own responses to violence and terror**
- **Understanding the teaching of Islam on violence**
- **Reflecting on how to live in peace**

Key questions

- **How should I respond to 11 September?**
- **How and why should we live in harmony?**

KEY WORDS

- **Harmony**
- **Mosque**
- **Peace**
- **Pentagon**
- **Salaam**

The World Trade Center

On 11 September 2001, four jet aircraft were hijacked from three different cities in the USA. The terrorists, who seemed to have taken over piloting the craft, had apparently planned suicide missions to crash these planes into important places along the east coast of America, including the World Trade Center and the **Pentagon**. In a matter of hours, more than 3,400 people had been killed. All over the world, people followed the horrifying events, often referred to since as 9/11, on radio and television.

Osama bin Laden

The terrorists who hijacked the planes were allegedly part of the al-Qaeda group led by Osama bin Laden. He said he wishes to remove non-Muslims from the Arab Peninsula and to unite Muslims against the policies of the western countries, especially the USA.

Following 11 September, in various parts of the world there were attacks on Muslims – **mosques** were vandalised, school buses stoned, people insulted. There are still people who blame all Muslims for the attacks.

OVER TO YOU

1 Ask your teacher what he or she can remember about the events of 9/11.

2 Carry out a survey among adults in your family about:

 a what they remember.
 b what their feelings were at the time.
 c who they think was to blame.

Bring together your findings and share them with the rest of the class.

3 a Using the weblinks suggested, research the facts about the events of that day.

 b What are your feelings after finding out more about what happened?

OVER TO YOU

4 'After our sister was killed on 9/11, we, individually and as a group, said that violent revenge for her death was not what we were calling for. We wanted justice; we wanted the perpetrators and their supporters identified, tried and legally punished.'

Not all people reacted like this. Do you think this is a good reaction? In small groups, discuss this reaction and explain your views.

Children's Express is a UK-wide news agency producing news, features and comment by young people for everyone. Shortly after the events of 9/11, a group of reporters from Children's Express went out onto the streets of Britain to ask young people what they thought. They were asked, 'Have the attacks on 11 September changed how people feel about Muslims?' Some of the responses are given in box **C**.

C

> I suppose, because they blame all of them, even though it was a group of people.

Rhian, 12

> Yes – people hate Muslims because Muslims hate all Christians. Not everyone, but some people do.

Tom, 15

Ed, 14

> Yeah, cause nobody likes Osama bin Laden, and he's Muslim.

Mari, 15

> I think it did because I think people blame all Muslims for the attacks they did – it's where it's heading back to, where the war is heading back to, to Islam. But it's only extremists, isn't it?

5 Read about Children's Express. What is your response to their question?

6 Using the weblinks suggested, find out more about Children's Express.

7 Think of other times when groups of people have been blamed because of the acts of a few.

8 Why do you think there is terrorism in the world?

9 In pairs, discuss the following possible responses to acts of terrorism and violence. Label them 'OK' or 'Not OK', and give your reasons why.

  a Judging people on how they look or dress.
  b Talking about how it feels to be a victim of violence or prejudice.
  c Thinking before you speak or act, especially when you are angry.
  d Verbal violence, including slurs, name calling and insults.
  e Making prejudiced comments or jokes about groups or individuals.
  f Helping victims to show your support.
  g Blaming people for the actions of others.
  h Celebrating the injury of innocent people.
  i Having some honest discussions about cultural differences.
  j Examining how television, music, newspapers and websites discuss religious issues.
  k Drawing or writing hateful symbols or words on your personal property.
  l Lashing out verbally at people who are different from you or whom you do not understand.

10 In pairs, create a 'Charter for understanding others'. Include in your charter things like 'Don't jump to conclusions' and 'Listen before you speak'.

11 Role play a conversation between a Muslim and a Christian about how to live together in harmony.

Let's reflect

The Arabic word for peace is '**salaam**' – the word that gives rise to the term 'Islam'. When Muslims greet one another, they say 'Peace be on you.'

'I'm a Muslim. I've been a Muslim for 20 years. I want the world to know the truth about Islam. I wouldn't be here to represent Islam if it were the way the terrorists make it look … Islam is for peace' (Muhammad Ali, former world heavyweight boxing champion).

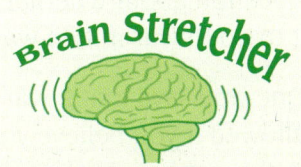

'We all lost a piece of our humanity on 11 September.'

What do you think this quote means? Do you agree with it?

WEBLINKS You will find links for this topic at www.nelsonthornes.com/exploringre

69

Is it right to go to war?

This is about ...

- **Understanding the idea of a just war**
- **Exploring some religious views on war**
- **Considering your own view about taking part in war**

Key questions

- **What do religious believers think about war?**
- **What do I believe about war?**

OVER TO YOU

1 Look carefully at photos **A–C** and identify which war is shown in each photo.

Look at photo **D**. What do you think is happening? Write a caption for this photo.

Many religious people of different faiths have answered the question about whether it is right to go to war in two ways:

- One way says that a war is allowed if you believe you are in the right.

- The other way says that any war or killing, no matter what the reason, is wrong in God's eyes – even in cases of self-defence.

KEY WORDS

- **Aggressor**
- **Buddha**
- **Compassion**
- **Just war**
- **Precept**

OVER TO YOU

2 In pairs, discuss the following scenarios. What would you do in each case?

a You are 18 and called to fight in a war.

b You are a soldier and ordered to attack a village that is hiding the enemy. There are women and children there.

c You are in the army and ordered to shoot at a group of enemy soldiers who do not know you are there.

d A group of enemy soldiers has burst into your platoon's camp.

e You are in the air force and ordered to bomb a factory near a school.

f You are a soldier and ordered to torture some prisoners to find out where they have taken your fellow comrades.

g You are in the army and ordered to kill a prisoner who, if he escapes, may give information leading to the death of hundreds of your comrades.

Over the years, a view has developed about what might be a **just war**. It is mainly a Christian idea, but other religions have similar views. It recognises three things: taking human life is seriously wrong; countries have a duty to defend their citizens; and sometimes violence has to be used to protect innocent human life and defend important moral values.

The principles of a just war are:

- the war must be for a just cause

- the war must be lawfully declared by a lawful authority

- the intention behind the war must be good

- all other ways of resolving the problem should have been tried first

- there must be a reasonable chance of success

- the means used must be in proportion to the end that the war seeks to achieve.

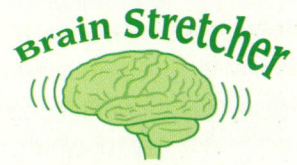

3 How many large-scale wars do you know about? Here are some from the last 50 years or so. Find out a little more about them, then carry out more detailed research into one of them and decide whether you think it was a just war.
  a Vietnam.
  b Kosovo.
  c The Falklands.
  d Afghanistan.
  e First Gulf War.
  f Iraq.

4 What do you think of the idea of a just war? In pairs, discuss the principles and give an example for each one.

5 Is there any moral difference between using ordinary weapons or nuclear weapons?

6 Should we ever bomb people who are not in the armed forces?

7 Is killing in a war any different from killing in everyday life?

8 Read the following Bible passages:
  a Matthew 5:38–39.
  b Matthew 21:12–13.
  c Matthew 26:52.

Imagine you are a Christian being interviewed on a radio station about your views on war. Write a script for the interview.

Here is a story from Buddhism. One day, Sinha, the general of the army, went to the **Buddha** and said, 'I am a soldier, O Blessed One. I am appointed by the king to enforce his laws and to wage his wars. The Buddha teaches infinite love, kindness and **compassion** for all sufferers. Does the Buddha permit the punishment of the criminal? And also, does the Buddha declare that it is wrong to go to war for the protection of our homes, our wives, our children and our property?'

The Buddha replied, 'He who deserves punishment must be punished. And he who is worthy of favour must be favoured. Do not do injury to any living being but be just, filled with love and kindness … When a magistrate punishes, he must not harbour hatred in his heart. When a murderer is put to death, he should realise that his punishment is the result of his own act.'

Let's reflect

Since 1945, there have been over 120 wars in the world. In the 1990s, more than one and half million people died in wars

Brain Stretcher

'You can be a soldier of truth, but not the **aggressor**' (Buddhist saying).

What do you think it means to be a 'soldier of truth'?

9 The first of the five Buddhist **precepts** is not to harm any living thing. How do you think this matches up with the advice from the Buddha?

10 Buddhists believe they should not even kill an insect. What do you think about this? How would this affect how Buddhists live their lives?

This is about ...

■ **Knowing what the six main religions teach about their approach to war**

■ **Understanding that there are differences of opinion within religions**

■ **Considering which views changed your thinking**

Key question

■ **What do the main religions teach about war?**

1 Read extracts **A–F** and then discuss them in a small group. Consider what each extract tells you about that religion's view on war, and then try to come to an agreement about whether in each religion war is:

a allowed.

b allowed in some circumstances.

c not allowed.

2 With a partner, discuss the views from each religion and identify something that really moved your thinking on or you liked very much. Use the light bulb test – what 'lit up' your thinking?

KEY WORDS

- **Ahimsa**
- **Compassion**
- **Harmony**
- **Holy war**
- **Injustice**
- **Jihad**
- **Just war**
- **Karma**
- **Martyr**
- **Messiah**
- **Pacifist**
- **Paradise**
- **Precept**
- **Qur'an**
- **Torah**

Help!

Light bulb test
Can you find an idea or a view to which you can give a light bulb? That means it lit up your thinking.

A

Buddhists must have **compassion** and not harm any living thing. The first of the five **precepts** is 'I will not harm any living thing.' Buddhists should not start a conflict even if it is to protect their religion. They must try to avoid any kind of violent act.

However, sometimes they may be forced to go to war by others who do not respect the way of the Buddha and may be called upon to defend their people from aggression. The Dalai Lama writes:

'All wars stem from our lack of human understanding, of mutual trust, and of mutual respect, based on kindness and love for all beings.'

B

In the New Testament, Jesus praised peacemakers, taught his followers not to take revenge, to love their enemies and to pray for those who persecute them:

'You have heard that it was said, "Eye for eye and tooth for tooth." But I tell you, do not resist an evil person. If someone strikes you on the right cheek, turn to him the other also' (Matthew 5:38–39).

'All who live by the sword will die by the sword' (Matthew 26:52).

However, in Luke 22, Jesus tells his disciples to arm themselves with a sword and seems to suggest they might need to defend themselves. He says:

'And if you don't have a sword, sell your cloak and buy one' (Luke 22.36).

Some Christians become **pacifists** but many would take part in a **just war**.

C The word 'Islam' has the idea of peace and when Muslims meet they say 'Peace be on you'. The Muslim word **jihad** means striving in the name of Allah. It does not mean **holy war** in the military sense, although the **Qur'an** allows war in defence of Islam:

'Strike terror into the enemy of God and your enemy … all that you give in the cause of God shall be repaid to you. You shall not be wronged' (Surah 8:61).

Indeed, the Qur'an says those who are killed in jihad are **martyrs** and will go to **paradise**. However, it also says that Muslims should make up their differences with others:

'Paradise is for those who curb their anger and forgive their fellow men' (Surah 3:134).

D For Jews, peace is very important and the Jewish greeting 'shalom' means 'peace be with you'. They look forward to the coming of the **Messiah**, which will be a time of peace and **harmony**. The dream is that:

'They will beat their swords into ploughshares … nation will not lift up sword against nation' (Micah 4:3).

However, Jews will defend themselves although war is a last resort. In the **Torah**, Jews are told not to be afraid of war as God will be with them. Yet they must make offers of peace before they go to war and they must be careful not to cause damage to the environment.

E War has been waged in the traditions of Hinduism, especially in the face of evil and injustice. The Bhagavad Gita is a message to Arjuna, an Indian prince, when he hesitates to wage a war against his own family and friends. Krishna advises him that he should wage the war because it is part of his duty or **karma** and that he should not think of withdrawing from his responsibility out of fear or cowardice. However, the concept of **ahimsa** means non-violence and respecting all life. Non-violence became famous around the world during the British rule of India when Mahatma Gandhi used it to oppose the British. Hinduism believes that God himself reincarnates whenever there is evil on Earth to protect the weak. Therefore, war is justified when it is meant to protect yourself and the world from evil and injustice:

'O Kaunteya, if you are killed [in the battle] you will ascend to heaven. On the contrary if you win the war you will enjoy the comforts of earthly kingdom. Therefore get up and fight with determination' (Bhagavad Gita 2.37).

F In the time of its founder Guru Nanak in the sixteenth century, Sikhism was clearly a religion of peace. Guru Nanak wrote:

'No one is my enemy
No one is a foreigner
With all I am at peace
God within us renders us
Incapable of hate and prejudice.'

Yet from the time of the fifth Guru, Arjan Dev, Sikhs had to fight to defend their religion. The tenth Guru, Guru Gobind Singh, urged Sikhs to fight against oppression and formed the Khalsa. However, he made it clear that violence and war were to be the last resort, but emphasised that they should not be avoided if necessary:

'When all efforts to restore peace prove useless and no words avail, lawful is the flash of steel. It is right to draw the sword.'

Why are some people pacifists?

This is about ...

- **Learning about pacifism**
- **Understanding what pacifism has achieved**
- **Considering your views on non-violence**
- **Being able to meditate**

Key questions

- What is **pacifism**?
- Why is pacifism important for some people?

KEY WORDS

- Ahimsa
- Buddha
- Discrimination
- Nun
- Pacifism
- Pacifist
- Precept

Pacifists commit themselves to non-violence and achieve their goals only through non-violent resistance. They try to deal with situations in a peaceful manner.

A

Thich Nu Thanh Quang

OVER TO YOU

1 In pairs, discuss how you would deal with the following situations and how a pacifist might act.

a Someone threatens you with a knife.

b Someone tries to rob you in the street.

c Your brother or sister wants to play a violent video game.

d Your country is invaded by an evil dictator.

OVER TO YOU

2 Look at photo **A**. In small groups, discuss the following questions.

a What are your feelings about Thich Nu Thanh Quang?

b What do you think she achieved?

c What are your views about the Buddhist quote that it is 'better to be killed than to kill'?

d What occasions might there be when you think it would be better to take a non-violent approach?

e 'Pacifists are cowards.' How would you reply to someone who held that view?

In May 1966, Thich Nu Thanh Quang, a Buddhist **nun**, set herself on fire in the city of Hue in protest against the Vietnam War. Her death was followed by a demonstration of some 20,000 people in Saigon. There were eight other suicides by Buddhists throughout the major cities of Vietnam.

The first truly pacifist movement we know of is early Buddhism. The **Buddha** expected his followers to stop any act of violence toward their fellow creatures. However, despite the growth of Buddhism, pacifism was not widely practised in Buddhist societies in general.

Buddhism developed from the teachings of Siddhartha Gautama, who became the Buddha. He believed human suffering could be overcome by following a particular way of life. The first **precept** of Buddhism is not to harm any living thing (**ahimsa**) – Buddhists reject violence. Buddhism is clearly pacifist in its teaching, and many Buddhists say it is 'better to be killed than to kill'.

3 Read Gandhi's words in box **B**. Do you think he was right? Discuss this with a partner.

B

I object to violence because when it appears to do good, the good is only temporary; the evil it does is permanent.

Fantastic Facts

Three major world religions have their roots in India: Hinduism, Buddhism and Sikhism. Buddhism and Sikhism both grew from Hinduism. All three share the idea of ahimsa.

OVER TO YOU

4 Think of some occasions when, in your view, non-violence could be used successfully. Then think of some occasions when, in your view, non-violence would not work. Give reasons. You can use examples from your experience.

5 Try some meditation. Many people, including religious believers, use meditation to calm themselves, focus on love and kindness, and dissolve anger and hate. We can use it to relax our bodies and minds and become more peaceful.

C

Mahatma Gandhi

Help!

Stilling and meditation

Stilling is simply to be still and relaxed and meditation is to concentrate on something to help you think more deep

Mahatma Gandhi was born in 1869 to Hindu parents in western India. He is famous for his use of non-violence against social evils such as racial **discrimination** and against British rule in India.

When he was a lawyer in South Africa, Gandhi refused to co-operate with the racist laws and suffered imprisonment many times, where he was attacked and beaten by white South Africans. It was while in prison that he began to teach non-violent resistance to, and non-cooperation with, the South African authorities.

Gandhi became a leader in the struggle for independence against British rule. Again, he encouraged non-violent resistance and non-cooperation. His followers would sit down in the streets or refuse to buy British goods, and Gandhi often fasted as a way of protesting.

Let's reflect

'Hatred is never appeased by hatred in this world; it is appeased by love' (Dhammapada 1:5).

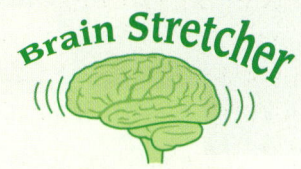

Brain Stretcher

'Pacifism does not mean passivism.'

What do you think this quote means?

In our journey through this unit, we have:

■ explored our views of the causes of violence

■ considered how we might react to violence against us

■ learned about the importance religion gives to forgiveness

■ examined how religion can cause war and make peace

■ studied the teachings of religions about taking part in war

■ reflected on what our views are about war and violence

Key questions

■ **How would people of different religions respond to situations of aggression?**

■ **What are my views about violence and war?**

KEY WORDS

- **Holy war**
- **Just war**
- **Pacifist**

1 Look at photo **A**, which shows a soldier in battle. Read the poem extract in box **B**. What do you think of the idea that God would protect a soldier in battle?

It could be argued that there are three possible views of war and violence that religious believers might have. These are:

● the **pacifist** view – all violence and killing is wrong

● the **just war** view – some wars and use of violence in some situations are right because they bring about justice

● the **holy war** view – God asks the believers to make war on those who do not believe in that religion or who are a threat to it.

A

B

My Son

I ask no honours on the field,
That other men have won as brave as he –
I only pray that God may shield
My son, and bring him safely back to me!

By Ada Tyrrell

2 In pairs, use what you have learned in this unit to tackle this task. Imagine a small country has been invaded by an evil dictator wanting to increase his territory. A United Nations task force is being assembled from a number of countries.

a The class will be divided into groups of six. In each group, each of you should take on the role of a representative from one of the major religions. Complete the speech bubble from the viewpoint of the religion you are representing. Discuss your opinions.

b What do you think about the views you have heard and what you have learned from them?

Let's reflect

'Whenever you are confronted with an opponent, conquer him with love' (Gandhi)

In his Sermon on the Mount (Matthew 5–7), Jesus said these words: 'You're blessed when you can show people how to co-operate instead of compete or fight. That's when you discover who you really are, and your place in God's family.' (From a modern version of the Bible called *The Message*.)

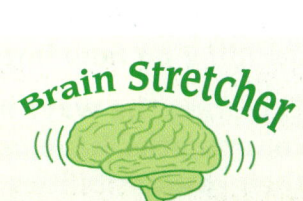

'*Religious conflict tells us less about religion and more about human nature.*'

What does this quote mean? Do you agree with it?

3 Name some peacemakers you know. They might be famous or from your community or circle of friends. Why do you regard them as peacemakers?

4 Think of times when you have been or wanted to be violent. What happened?

5 Think of times when you have been a peacemaker. What did you do? How did you feel?

6 You have considered and discussed the views of the main religions about violence and war. What are your views?

This is about

- **Considering** what you are entitled to as a human being

- **Understanding** that your rights carry responsibilities

- **Analysing** different worlds and communities and deciding on their importance they are to you

- **Exploring** the ways in which different faith communities have promoted human rights and taken their responsibilities seriously

- **Reflecting on what is most important to you in life**

- **Considering and expressing your views on the issues discussed**

Key questions

- What are **human rights**?

- What rights do I have?

- Which of my rights are most important to me?

- What are my **responsibilities** towards others?

- In what ways do religious people respond to their responsibilities?

KEY WORDS

- **Community**
- **Curfews**
- **Human rights**
- **Responsibilities**

From the BBC News website (news.bbc.co.uk), 18 September 2004

In this unit we will be considering what rights we have or are entitled to. We will also be looking at the idea that along with rights go responsibilities – to ourselves and to others. Faith communities take great care of their members from childhood and also show concern for others when they work in the **community**. We shall also be thinking about those whose rights are often denied.

OVER TO YOU

1 Read the newspaper article in box **A**.

a Why do you think a curfew has been imposed?

b Do you agree with the idea of the curfew? Explain why.

c Does the boy have any rights about this?

Teenager to challenge curfew law

A

A teenager is set to legally challenge new powers allowing police and councils in England and Wales to impose night-time **curfews** on children aged under 16.

Lawyers for the boy believe the powers in the Anti-Social Behaviour Act are in breach of his human rights.

The boy, 14, has been granted legal aid to take the case to the High Court.

Under the new rules, police can escort home anyone under 16 who is unsupervised in a designated area after 9.00 pm. They have the authority to escort children home from the areas even if they have done nothing wrong.

A curfew is in force in Richmond-upon-Thames around the town centre and riverbank. By introducing the measure in July, local authorities wanted to ensure that visitors and ordinary people going about their everyday lives did not feel intimidated by groups of mainly young people, said Mr Arbour, leader of Richmond-upon-Thames council.

2 Imagine you have been shipwrecked on a remote island with a small number of other people you were sailing with. There is no way you will be rescued, so you know you need to start a new community. As well as making a set of rules by which to live, you also need to decide what rights every individual will have. These rights need to ensure everyone lives happily and to help you all live peacefully. In small groups, brainstorm a list of about ten rights that you want to give everyone in your community.

3 Feed back your list to the rest of the class. Compare the different ideas you have all come up with. How many similar ideas have been thought of?

4 In your groups, make any changes to your list of rights.

5 Share your final list with the rest of the class and try to make a list that the whole class is happy with.

All human beings agree that there are certain aspects of life we are all entitled to. These are called our human rights. On 10 December 1948, 51 countries from around the world signed the Universal Declaration of Human Rights. This document sets out a list of rights we all have and share with others around the world. Having these rights does not depend on where you live, what colour your skin is or how old you are.

The declaration is made up of 30 statements describing everyone's human rights. You can read some of the main ones in box **B**.

B

1 No one should be held in slavery.
2 No one should be tortured.
3 Everyone has the right to freedom of opinion and expression of that opinion in any way they wish.
4 All human beings are born free and equal and should treat all people as if they are brothers.
5 Everyone has the right to a standard of living that allows for good health.
6 Everyone has the right to wellbeing including food, clothing, housing and medical care.
7 Everyone has the right to be taken care of if they are unemployed, sick, disabled, widowed, old or unable to look after themselves.
8 Everyone has the right to freedom of thought, conscience and religion.
9 Everyone has the right to education.

From the Universal Declaration of Human Rights

6 Look at the rights in box **B**. Which rights do you think are the most important? Write them down in a diamond nine shape. The right in the top diamond is the most important, and the one in the bottom diamond is the least important.

7 In small groups, choose one of the rights in box **B** and think of examples where these rights:

   a are being allowed.
   b are not being given.

Help!

Diamond nine activities

This is an activity where a list of things is rearranged in order of priority. The most important thing is placed at position 1. Continue to prioritise each item in the list until the least important is placed at position 9. You can do this on your own or in groups. In groups you will need to discuss your choices to reach a joint decision.

You will find links for this topic at
www.nelsonthornes.com/exploringre

This is about ...

- Understanding what rights you have and why you have them
- Empathising with those who have few or no rights
- Learning about a religious organisation that supports children's rights

Key questions

- Do I have any rights?
- Do all children and young people enjoy the same rights?
- Do religions do anything about this?

KEY WORDS

- Advocacy
- Discrimination
- Hostage

In September 2004, terroris[ts hel]d over 1,000 pupils and teach[ers] **hostage** at a school in Bes[lan,] Russia. The siege ended wit[h over] 300 people dead, 150 of the[m] children.

OVER TO YOU

1 Look at photo **A**, which [...]

  a What are your feeli[ngs ...]

  b Why do you think t[...]

  c Why do you think [...] children were killed?

2 In most countries, children have always been specially protected and cared for. What rights do you think children in the UK should have?

  a Copy and complete the charter below.

Children's charter
I have the right to...
I have the right to...
I have the right to...
I have the right to...
I have the right to...

  b Why do you think you should have these rights?

3 Do you know what you can do legally at different ages? In pairs, try to decide at what age you are legally allowed to the following. (The answers are given at the bottom of page 81.)

  a Can be convicted of a criminal offence.

  b Can hold a driving licence.

  c Can join the army.

  d Can get a part-time job.

  e Can hold a full passport.

  f Can be convicted of rape (boy).

The United Nations Convention on the Rights of the Child was passed in 1990. Box **B** outlines some of its main features.

B

1 Children shall be entitled to be healthy and have adequate diet, housing, recreation and medical services.

2 Children need love and understanding, affection, security and dignity.

3 Children are entitled to receive free education.

4 Children shall have full opportunity for play and recreation.

5 Children shall be among the first to receive protection and relief.

6 Children shall be protected against all forms of neglect, cruelty and exploitation.

7 Children shall be protected from practices that may foster racial, religious and any other form of **discrimination**.

From the UN Convention on the Rights of the Child

4 Read the rights of the child in box **B**. How important do you think these rights are? Place them on a continuum from 'Really important' to 'Not important'.

```
|_____|
```

Really important   **Not important**

C

I wasn't able to stay on at school because my parents couldn't afford the cost, because some days we only have enough to eat for one meal. I go out begging not because I want to but because I don't have any choice at the moment. I go to the Bar Bozo and wait for what's left over from the tourists' meals so that I can fill my stomach, even if it's no good. What's important is to fill my stomach, never mind anything else. In the future I'd like to become a fisherman, in order to earn my living and help those who haven't got enough, with the poverty that exists here, and the endless hardship of living in the town. I know I'm not going to stay like this; if I do I'll have no dignity. We are all poor and unworthy but we love one another.

By Sanousi Diarra, aged 10

Help!

Continuums

A continuum is a line along which you decide to place a word or idea and then discuss your decision with others.

5 Read the words of Sanousi Diarra in box **C**, a boy who lives in a town called Mopti in Mali, west Africa.

a Which of the rights listed in box **B** does Sanousi not have?

b How does Sanousi's life compare with yours? Use the living graph technique to plot your life compared to Sanousi's.

Help!

Living graphs

A living graph has two axes. One is a timeline and the other shows, for example, people's feelings. Often you will be given pieces of 'evidence' such as letters or statements, which are cut out and placed where you think they should go on a blank graph outline.

```
|
|
|
|_____
          Time
```

TEARFUND
CHRISTIAN ACTION WITH THE WORLD'S POOR

How do religions help children gain their rights? Tearfund is a Christian charity that works with the world's poorest communities to forge ways out of poverty. Jesus said he came to bring 'life in all its fullness' and Tearfund says its vision is to see lives transformed – economically, physically and spiritually.

Through smaller 'partner' organisations operate in more than 70 countries, Tearfund addresses long-term needs such as employment, healthcare and education. Emergency teams supply food and medicines after disasters, and **advocacy** specialists lobby politicians to make decisions that are fair to people in poor countries.

Charles Samson, 15, from Malawi, started begging after his mum died. A children's drop-in centre that Tearfund supports invited him in and found him a carpentry apprenticeship. He used to be aggressive but now he is relaxed and helpful, and excited about his future.

6 Imagine you are Charles. Write a paragraph about what your life is like at the moment.

What responsibilities do I have?

This is about ...

- **Understanding that with rights come responsibilities towards others**
- **Analysing different responsibilities and deciding on how important they are**
- **Considering what responsibilities religions have and why**

OVER TO YOU

1. What responsibilities do you have, at school, at home, towards your friends, towards your family and neighbours? You are going to use the zoom lens board strategy for this activity. Write each responsibility on a small card or piece of paper. Consider how important each responsibility is before placing each card in the appropriate circle of a zoom lens board. Explain your views.

2. On the back of each card, add consequences to your responsibilities. A consequence is the result of either doing something or not. What would be the consequences of not carrying out your duties and responsibilities?

Key questions

- **What are my responsibilities towards others?**
- **In what ways do religious people respond to their responsibilities?**

KEY WORDS

- **Gurdwara**
- **Human rights**
- **Ramadan**
- **Responsibilities**

> As I'm a Christian, during Christian Aid week I get involved in sponsored events and try to raise money to help people who don't have all the things I take for granted sometimes.
>
> **Ceri**

> As a Buddhist, being concerned about those who suffer and need help is important. Giving and working for charity, and helping others, helps me to remember this every day. Once a week, I lead meditation sessions to help people who are coming off drugs.
>
> **Surana**

Help!

Zoom lens boards

A zoom lens board is five concentric circles on a large piece of paper. The central circle represents 'Most important', the second circle 'Very important', the third circle 'Important', the fourth circle 'Fairly important' and the fifth circle 'Least important'.

Least important
Fairly important
Important
Very important
Most important

Considering the consequences should help us understand how important our responsibilities are towards others. If we did not have our **human rights** protected in law, our lives would be difficult. However, if we want to have our rights, we also have a responsibility towards others. Most people would agree that those of us who enjoy our human rights have a responsibility to help those who do not.

What do religions teach about responsibilities? All religions teach their followers that we have a responsibility to help others in need, especially if we are safe and cared for. Here are some views from teenagers who act upon their religious teachings, and some quotes from the scriptures (box **A**).

*Seeing all the images of bombed towns and villages in the Iraq War made me feel terrible for my fellow brothers and sisters in other parts of the Muslim world. I completed a sponsored swim. I raised about £70. I'll be praying hard and thinking carefully about Muslims in need during **Ramadan** this year.*

Amir

I'm a Hindu, so, through donations to the Hare Krishna Food for Life charity organisation, I sponsor a little girl called Priya in a small village in Rajput. The money I send helps her get an education so she won't have to go into child slavery.

Ashoki

*I'm a Sikh. I helped to set up an emergency appeal at our local **gurdwara** to help people affected by the Bangladeshi floods recently. By serving others in this way, I'm also serving God.*

Sharonjit

'Most of us can read the writing on the wall; we just assume it's addressed to someone else' (Ivern Ball, American writer, b1926).

What do you think this quote has to do with your study of responsibilities?

I was always involved in helping fundraising for Tzedek when I was still at home. When I came to university, I set up the youth group and now we have a fundraising event every month.

Daniel

3 **a** From the information in box **A** and the teenagers' words above, match up the religious teaching to their actions.

b Explain how each person does something responsible towards others. What are the long-term consequences of their actions?

A

The riches of those who are generous never waste away, while those who will not give find none to comfort them. (Rig Veda 10:117)

It is righteous to … spend of your substance out of love for [Allah], for your kin, for orphans, for the needy, for the wayfarer. (Surah 2:177)

He secures justice for those who are wronged and gives food for the hungry. (Psalm 146:7)

Our service in the world gets us a seat in the Court of the Lord. (Guru Nanak)

I was hungry and you gave me food, I was thirsty and you gave me drink, I was a stranger and you welcomed me. (Matthew 25:40)

A person must be generous in giving what his friend needs; must talk with his friend courteously; must look after his friend's well being. (the Buddha)

What responsibilities do religions have and why?

This is about ...

- Understanding the responsibilities that religions believe they have towards others
- Understanding why religions would want to help others
- Identifying the different ways that religious organisations support human rights
- Exploring the projects of various religious organisations

Key questions

- How do religious people help others in need?
- Why would religious people want to help others?

KEY WORDS

- Community
- Human rights
- Responsibilities
- Volunteers

Showing concern for others is an important part of religious life for many followers of a religious faith. Failing to help others in need is believed to disappoint God himself, and stops us from being true human beings ourselves.

The organisations on these pages all carry out projects around the world that support people whose human rights are being affected. By fulfilling their duties to help others, they are fulfilling the wishes of God. The founders of religions – such as Jesus, Guru Nanak and the Prophet Muhammad – have themselves set examples of how to live in the world with others, and believers try to follow the example of the founder of their religion.

Recall ...

Why is it important to carry out our **responsibilities** towards others? Remind yourself about what we mean by the word 'responsibility'. We will be trying to work out how religious organisations help those who are denied some of their human rights.

OVER TO YOU

1. Look at the logos of different organisations in box **A**.
   a. Which religions are represented here?
   b. What do their logos tell you about each organisation?

B

Learning a skill with Tzedek

Tzedek is a Jewish overseas development and educational charity based in the UK and founded in 1990. It works with people from all races and religions who are from some of the poorest **communities** of the world. Its aim is to help the people help themselves and relieve their poverty.

Katie Schenk and Judy Sender, former **volunteers** with Tzedek, visited Tzedek's project in Sri Lanka where they were working with street children and their families. This is what they wrote in their diary:

While travelling through Sri Lanka we paid a visit to the Borela Centre, which has been set up to help Colombo's street children and their families. We were taken to the centre by two of the staff members. The centre offers a range of services and facilities for up to 50 families who live on the streets. The centre has a pre-school, women's and a teenage education and skills project. All the centre's members are provided with a full and nutritious meal each day.

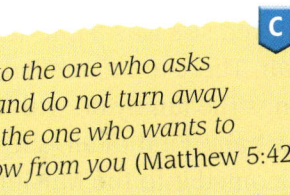
OVER TO YOU

2 Why would Jewish people want to get involved in Tzedek?

3 Read the quotes in **C**. Why would religious people want to help others whose rights are being denied?

C

Give to the one who asks you, and do not turn away from the one who wants to borrow from you (Matthew 5:42).

The Lord … watches over the stranger; the Lord gives heart to the orphan and the widow (Psalm 146:9).

Allah requires justice and kindness and generosity (Surah 16:90).

I am the friend of all people, the companion of all people. I sympathise with all living beings. I cultivate a compassionate mind and rejoice in not harming living creatures (Thera Gatha, a Buddhist sacred text).

Serve God. Serve humanity. Only service to humanity shall secure for us a place in heaven (Guru Nanak).

OVER TO YOU

4 Using the weblinks suggested, choose one of the following websites. Find a project to research and design a leaflet explaining the organisation's work, the responsibilities it has, and why this work is important in supporting **human rights**.

a Christian Aid.
b Tearfund.
c Muslim Aid.
d Tzedek.
e Trek-Aid.
f Sewa International.
g Khalsa Aid.

Your leaflet needs to show the information in an easy-to-read format, with pictures to back up your facts. It could be an A4 piece of paper folded into three. This will give you space for a front cover, where you can put the organisation's name and logo. The information can be set in bullet points inside.

WEBLINKS You will find links for this topic at www.nelsonthornes.com/exploringre

How important are children in religion?

This is about ...

- **Understanding the ceremonies in which two faith communities welcome children into the world**
- **Considering the importance of names in some faith communities**
- **Reflecting on the way in which religious ceremonies show the importance of children**

Key questions

- How do religions celebrate the birth of a baby?
- How important are children in a religious home?

KEY WORDS

- **Adhan**
- **Aqiqah**
- **Aum**
- **Community**
- **Karma**
- **Mandir**
- **Muhammad**
- **Prophet**
- **Responsibilities**
- **Samskara**

Children are very important to all religions. They have rights and **responsibilities**. In Islam, children are entitled to various rights. The first and foremost of these is to be raised and educated properly. They should be taught true values, the meaning of right and wrong, true and false. The **Prophet Muhammad** said, 'A man is like a shepherd of his own family, and he is responsible for them.' Children, therefore, are given on trust given to their parents. They are to be well-fed, properly dressed and filled with faith, knowledge and wisdom.

Mr and Mrs Ahmed were delighted with the birth of their daughter, and, like all Muslims, believed she was a gift from Allah. There are a number of things the family do with their new baby. First of all, she is welcomed into the Muslim community with the words of the Muslim call to prayer, the **adhan**. These words are whispered into the baby's right ear by her father. The words are:

'God is great, there is no God but Allah. Muhammad is the messenger of Allah. Come to prayer. Come to success. God is great. There is no God but Allah.'

This means that the name of Allah is the first word the new baby hears. The baby's first taste should be something sweet, so parents may chew a piece of date and rub the juice along her gums.

After seven days, family and friends gather for the **aqiqah**, when the baby's head is shaved to show that she is the servant of Allah. The hair is weighed and the equivalent weight in silver is given by the family to charity.

A

An animal is sacrificed in thanksgiving for the gift of a child from Allah (in Britain this takes place at an abattoir). Afterwards, the meat is cooked and some is given to the poor.

The baby is also given a name, chosen by the parents. They might choose a family name, or one that is linked to Allah, or one of the names of the prophets or messengers of Allah.

Fantastic Facts

In Islam, Allah has 99 names, each one describing a different characteristic. Examples include 'the Merciful', 'the Holy One', 'the Truth'.

OVER TO YOU

1. What do you understand by Mr and Mrs Ahmed's daughter being described as a 'gift from Allah'?

2. If you were a parent, how would you choose your baby's name?

3. How did your parents decide what to call you?

4. Using the weblinks suggested, find out the meaning of your name and those of your friends.

5. Christians sometimes choose their children's names from the Bible. Sometimes they name them after a famous Christian from the past.

   a Find out what each of the following names mean.

   b Which ones do you like? Explain why.

   Boys: Adam, Christopher, David, Francis, Jonathan, Luke, Matthew, Michael, Paul.

   Girls: Anna, Bernadette, Chloë, Deborah, Faith, Grace, Lydia, Mary, Teresa.

6. Muslim boys are often named after one of Allah's messengers, most commonly Muhammad. The girls are often named after one of his wives or daughters. Here is a list of Muslim names and their meanings. Which ones do you like? Explain why.

   Boys: Abdul (slave), Bashir (bringer of good news), Dalil (guide), Habib (beloved), Hasan (handsome), Khalil (intimate friend).

   Girls: Arifa (knowledgeable), Bahija (happy), Dunya (life), Falilah (successful), Ghufran (forgiveness), Hakimah (wise).

Like any other Hindu family, Mr and Mrs Patel were overjoyed at the birth of their son. **Samskaras** are ceremonies that are held to mark a new stage in life. Hindus believe there are up to 16 samskaras in life, some of which take place before birth.

When the baby is born, a ceremony called Jatakarma is performed to welcome him into the family and the world. After being washed, the holy symbol **Aum** is written in honey on his tongue with a special golden pen.

About 12 days after birth, the baby is given his name. The baby's name is important – it is often the name of a god or a relative, or it describes what his parents want him to be like. The priest studies the baby's horoscope and suggests what the first letter of his name should be. Mr and Mrs Patel named their son Amit, which means 'lovable'.

Later in his first year, Amit will have his head shaved. This removes bad **karma** from his previous life. The ceremony will take place in the **mandir** with all the family present.

B

OVER TO YOU

7. Design and create an invitation to the ceremony when Amit's head will be shaved.

8. What do you think about the Hindu belief in karma?

9. What do these pages tell you about the importance of children in faith communities?

10. Think of other birth ceremonies you have learned about. How are they similar? What differences are there?

WEBLINKS You will find links for this topic at www.nelsonthornes.com/exploringre

Who cares about refugees and asylum seekers?

This is about ...

- **Understanding the problems faced by refugees and asylum seekers**
- **Clarifying your feelings about the issues**
- **Considering the views and activities of some religious people**

Key questions

- Why do people care about **refugees** and **asylum seekers**?
- In what ways have religious people responded to these issues?

KEY WORDS

- **Asylum seeker**
- **Communist**
- **Compassion**
- **Mercy**
- **Persecute**
- **Refugee**

Who are these people and what do they have in common? (The answers are given at the bottom of page 89.)

OVER TO YOU

1. What is the difference between a refugee and an asylum seeker?

2. Look at the refugee family in photo **E**. In pairs, discuss what kinds of problems they are likely to meet.

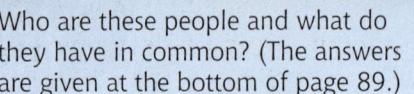

One in five flock here; asylum: we're too damn soft

From the Daily Star, 23 January 2004

Some people leave their home and country because of war, or because they are being persecuted for what they believe or what religion or race they belong to. Many of these people come to the UK for safety – they seek 'asylum'. Some people in the UK are against asylum seekers coming here.

A refugee family

4 Read the newspaper article in box **F**.

a What are you feelings about this situation?

b Do you think the UK government should help them? If so, how?

F

Mongolian family refused asylum

A Mongolian family based in Liverpool have been told they will be deported, just days after their daughter was princess of the Lord Mayor's Parade.

The Narantsogts have had two previous applications for asylum refused and were detained for two weeks at Dungavel immigration centre in Lanarkshire. Their lawyer, Aamer Anwar, says he has 'fresh evidence' the family will be in danger if they are sent home.

'We are lodging documents with the Home Office of proof that this family are exposed to the high risks of persecution if they are returned,' he said.

Jugder, 38, Shinee, 37, and children Evsaana, 17, and Misheel, aged 8, had been living in Liverpool before they were taken to Dungavel on 3 June. The family fled Mongolia two years ago after Mr Narantsogt was arrested for opposing the ruling **Communist** Party.

From the BBC News website (news.bbc.co.uk), 19 July 2004

Jesus told his followers to 'love your neighbour as yourself' (Matthew 25:29–31). In a modern version of the Bible, *The Message*, we read, 'Keep on loving each other as brothers. Do not forget to entertain strangers' (Hebrews 13:1–2).

Many Jewish laws and traditions are concerned with the poor, widows, orphans, travellers and others in need. It is a Jewish tradition to give hospitality to travellers and strangers. Jews understand God as a God of **compassion** and **mercy**:

'For the Lord your God is … the awesome God who does not show partiality … He brings about justice for the orphan and the widow, and shows his love for the stranger by giving him food and clothing. Therefore, show your love for the stranger' (Deuteronomy. 10:17–19).

Embrace is a group of Christians who have come together to support asylum seekers and refugees in Northern Ireland. Their aims are to tell people about the problems of those who are asylum seekers and to involve the local community in helping them. They have drawn up a list of things to do to make asylum seekers feel more welcome:

● Meet their eyes, smile at them and greet them when you meet.

● If someone comes to live in your street, call in and welcome them.

● Invite them for a meal in your home.

● Take time to understand accents which are different from our own.

● Challenge yourself and family about your attitudes to those who are different.

● Ask people from other countries about what their home is like.

5 Read the list that Embrace has drawn up. Add some other points that you think are important in helping asylum seekers feel welcome.

Answers They were all refugees. **A** Albert Einstein (1879–1955), German-Jewish physicist who fled from Nazi Germany to the UK then the USA; **B** Dalai Lama (b1935), Tibetan Buddhist leader. When Tibet was invaded by China, he fled to Nepal where he now lives as a refugee; **C** Jesus Christ. His family fled with him as a baby from Israel to Egypt.

WEBLINKS You will find links for this topic at www.nelsonthornes.com/exploringre

Should I aim to be rich?

This is about ...

- **Understanding that your attitudes shape the way you live**
- **Reflecting on what your attitude is to wealth**
- **Exploring how important wealth is to religious people**

Key questions

- **What is most important in my life?**
- **Do I have a responsibility to others?**

KEY WORDS

- **Qur'an**
- **Responsibility**
- **Shabbat**
- **Zakah**

OVER TO YOU

2 Read what the people in box **G** are saying about their attitudes to happiness and success. In pairs, discuss your views about what they are saying.

3 a Read the teachings in boxes **H**, **I** and **J**. They explain what three religions – Islam, Hinduism and Judaism – teach about wealth.

b Based on what you have learned, explain in your own words what each religious follower is saying.

OVER TO YOU

1 Look at photos **A–F** and decide how important each item shown is to you. Place them on a continuum of 'Really important' to 'Not important'.

```
Really                    Not
important              important
```

Some human rights laws include the right to work, the right to have enough food and clothes, and the right to have a place to live. You probably agree that these things are essential. However, how important is it to have lots of money? Should we all be aiming to get rich? Do we have responsibilities towards those in the developing world?

Help!

Continuums
A continuum is a line along which you decide to place a word or idea and then discuss your decision with others.

G

I think life is about getting as much money as possible and then spending it.

All I want is a gorgeous guy and a big house.

It seems to me that the more money people have, the more they want.

You should always give to someone in need.

You can tell whether someone's successful by how much money they have in the bank.

H

Muslims believe that whatever wealth and property they have comes from Allah, and 2.5% of their savings should go to the poor (**Zakah**). In the **Qur'an**, we read, 'And there are those who hoard gold and silver and spend it not in the way of Allah; announce unto them a most grievous chastisement' (Surah 9:34).

Wealth should not be in the hands of a few but flow through society to break down the differences between rich and poor.

Islam

I

For Hindus, wealth can be enjoyed and becoming rich is not a sin. However, to use it just for yourself and your own family is wrong. In the Bhagavad Gita, Krishna warns, 'He who eats all by himself without first offering to others eats only sin.' However much a Hindu earns, only that which is needed for the basic things in life should be kept.

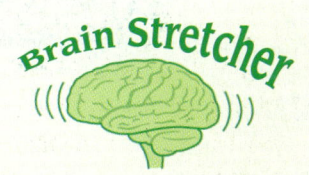

Hinduism

Jews believe that all they have belongs to God. They are expected to give a tenth of their wealth to the poor as charity, which they do at special occasions such as **Shabbat** and the Jewish festivals. The Jewish Rabbi Maimonides wrote, 'Who is rich? He who is satisfied with what he has.'

J

Judaism

Brain Stretcher

'The real measure of your wealth is how much you'd be worth if you lost all your money.'

What do you think this quote means? Do you agree with it?

Faith CONNECTIONS

Read the story of Guru Nanak and Duni Chand on the website. What attitude to wealth can you find there?

WEBLINKS You will find links for this topic at www.nelsonthornes.com/exploringre

Do animals have rights?

This is about ...

- **Examining opinions about the way animals should be treated**
- **Understanding that in religious belief animals are important beings that deserve fair treatment**
- **Expressing your own opinions on the ways animals should be treated**

Key questions

- **How should I treat animals?**
- **What is the attitude of religions to animals?**

KEY WORDS

- Ahimsa
- Buddha
- Francis of Assisi
- Muhammad
- Prophet
- Responsibility

A

The RSPCA is calling for a ban on all battery cages. Around 21 million hens are living in battery cages with almost no space to stretch their wings, move around properly or behave naturally.

A teenager from Tyne and Wear has been banned from keeping animals for five years after she starved a puppy close to death.

Hunting with dogs came to an end as MPs voted by an overwhelming majority to pass the Hunting Bill. Hunting with dogs for animals such as foxes, deer and mink ended in February 2005.

An adventurous hedgehog was recovered at the RSPCA's Norfolk Wildlife Centre after being rescued from a watery grave in the murky River Wensum in Norwich.

Fantastic Facts

In 2003, RSPCA inspectors investigated 105,932 animal cruelty complaints, which resulted in 1,829 convictions.

Most people agree that animals have thoughts and feelings. Think about how animals react when they feel threatened or are shown affection. They can learn certain habits, perform courageous deeds and respond to both kindness and cruelty. Many animals also rely on human beings to help them survive.

OVER TO YOU

1   Read the newspaper articles in box **A**.
   a   What are your feelings when you read these news stories?
   b   On a card, write down some of your feelings and read them to the rest of the class.

2   Have you ever owned a pet? List five rules for all pet owners.

3   a   What feelings do humans have towards animals?
   b   Do humans feel the same way about all animals?

4   What animals do you like and dislike? Explain why.

5   In what ways do you think humans and animals are similar or different? Use a Venn diagram to record your ideas.

Help!

Venn diagrams
Venn diagrams show what things have in common, and what the differences are.

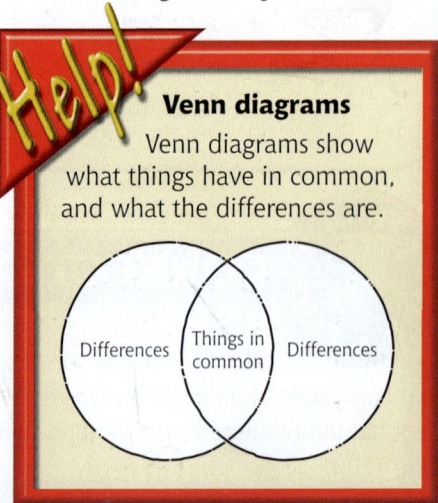

Differences | Things in common | Differences

The **Prophet Muhammad** showed great love and respect for animals. He was walking around teaching the people of Madinah. It was very hot, and many were sitting in the shade to avoid the baking sun. As he passed through a garden, his attention was caught by the great, pitiful howling sound of a camel. As Muhammad looked more closely at the camel, he could see that it was tied to a post, in full glare of the sun. It was very thin and obviously hungry and thirsty. He went over to the animal and dried its tears. The beast quietened.

Muhammad looked around the garden for the camel's owner. When he found him, Muhammad told him that he had been cruel to the animal by making it work hard and by not caring for it. The man was ashamed. He had been cool, comfortable and happy while his camel was hot, bothered and upset. From that day on, the camel owner looked after his animals with great care, and always made sure they had enough to eat and drink. The camel never cried again. The Prophet explained that all animals are God's creatures. Allah is pleased when his creatures are treated well, but angry if they are treated badly.

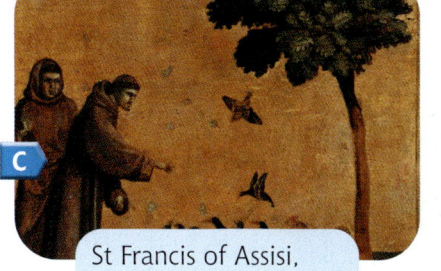

St Francis of Assisi, preaching to the birds

Father **Francis of Assisi** and his companions were walking through a valley. Suddenly, Francis spotted a great number of birds. There were doves, crows and all sorts of birds. Swept up in the moment, Francis left his friends in the road and ran after the birds, who waited patiently for him. He greeted the birds in his usual way, expecting them to fly off into the air as he spoke. But they did not move.

Amazed, he asked the birds if they would stay and listen to the word of God. He said to them:

'My brother and sister birds, you should praise your creator and always love him: he gave you feathers for clothes, wings to fly and all other things that you need. It is God who made you noble among all creatures, making your home in thin, pure air. Without sowing or reaping, you receive God's guidance and protection.'

Then he gave them his blessing, making the sign of the cross over them. At that, they flew off and Francis, rejoicing and giving thanks to God, went on his way.

OVER TO YOU

6 Read the stories about Muhammad and St Francis. In small groups, discuss what you think Muslims and Christians believe about how animals should be treated.

CONNECTIONS

- For Jews and Christians, the creation story shows how human beings were given rule over the animals, but they were also given a **responsibility** for caring for and not exploiting animals.

- In Buddhism, the teachings of the **Buddha** make it clear that no living creature should be harmed, showing a deep concern for the wellbeing of all animals.

- For Hindus, **ahimsa** (non-violence and respect for life) is extremely important. All life is sacred and this applies to all forms including fish, birds, mammals and insects. In the cycle of birth, death and rebirth, all living things need to be treated with the same amount of respect.

OVER TO YOU

7 In small groups, role play a meeting where the following topics will be discussed:
   a Blood sports.
   b Vegetarianism.
   c Experimenting on animals.

Each member of your group should take on the role of a religious believer.

8 In pairs, create a 'Charter for animal rights'. Base this on your views as a result of your role play in task 7.

 **WEBLINKS** You will find links for this topic at www.nelsonthornes.com/exploringre

Human rights and responsibilities

In our journey through this unit, we have:

■ explored our rights and responsibilities

■ examined what the attitudes of religious groups are to these issues

Key questions

■ **What are my responsibilities towards other people?**

■ **In what ways should religious people respond to their responsibilities?**

KEY WORDS

• **Responsibility**

Photo **A** shows the tragic scene in which a woman was left lying in the road after being attacked. The picture was taken by the onboard camera of a bus travelling along the busy Cray Road in Foots Cray, Kent, on 20 September 2004, just after 2 pm. Drivers are seen on the bus's CCTV footage swerving to avoid the woman, who was bleeding heavily from a wound to her head. Incredibly, none of them stopped. Lots of cars drove by, ignoring the woman. The driver of the bus stopped and protected her from oncoming traffic by positioning the bus behind her. He then called the police.

The injured woman lies unconscious in the road

This incident poses some questions, such as:

● What rights does the woman have?

● What is the **responsibility** of the car drivers?

● Why should anyone do anything to help the woman?

● Is it more or less likely that a religious person would help than a non-religious person?

OVER TO YOU

1 Look at photo **A** and read what happened.

  a What is your response to the story?

  b Why do you think the cars did not stop?

  c What would you have done?

2 Read the story of the good Samaritan in the Bible (Luke 10:25–37). What are the similarities and differences between these stories?

OVER TO YOU

3 In pairs, answer the questions raised above.

4 Can you think of any other questions that arise from the incident?

5 Two men were in a rowing boat. One began to saw a hole in the boat under his feet. When challenged by the other, he said, 'I have a right to cut this hole since this spot beneath my feet belongs to me.' The man replied, 'But if you continue, you will sink both of us since we are in this boat together.' In small groups, discuss how this story makes a comment on what we have been studying in this unit.

Bono, the lead singer of the band U2, has strong views as a Christian, especially about the way people have reacted slowly to the Aids crisis in Africa. To get the attention of Christians, Bono taped a three-minute video for artists to play at Christian music festivals. In the video, he asks the audience to write to political leaders to express their desire to make Aids and poverty in Africa a priority. You can read more of what he says in box **B**.

B

Today – in the next 24 hours – 5,500 Africans will die of Aids. Today, in childbirth, 1,400 African mothers will pass on HIV to their newborns. If this isn't an emergency, what is? In the scriptures we are not advised to love our neighbour, we are commanded. The Church needs to lead the way here, not drag its heels. The government needs guidance. We discuss, we debate, we put our hands in our pockets. We are generous even. But, I tell you, God is not looking for alms [charity], God is looking for action.

6 Read Bono's words in box **B**. What kind of action is he is suggesting?

7 Find some U2 songs that have a message like this in them.

8 Write a short song with the same theme.

9 If people lived up to the responsibilities that Bono is talking about, what do you think would happen in the world?

10 What have you learned in this unit?
   a Complete a large copy of the learning graph below to show where you have learned most.
   b In pairs, discuss what you have learned at those times.
   c Discuss in what ways you have learned most.

A lot ┤

Not a lot └──
       Unit 1   Unit 2   Unit 3   Unit 4   Unit 5
       Strereotyping, Freedom and Being   Violence, war Human rights
       prejudice and justice   commited   and peace   and
       discrimination   responsibilities

12 Below are some of the main concepts, questions and issues we have looked at in this unit. Tackle this task in pairs.

   a Copy each concept onto a separate piece of paper measuring about 5 cm x 5 cm.
   b On a clean piece of A4 paper, draw a cross to divide it into quarters.
   c In each quarter, write one of these headings: Big action, Some action, Little action, No action.
   d Take each concept in turn and place it in one of the quarters, depending on the kind of action you think we need to take in society. Discuss why you have chosen to place it there.
   e As a result of your conversations, you might decide to move the concept to another quarter.

| HUMAN RIGHTS |
| MY RIGHTS |
| MY RESPONSIBILITIES |
| CHILDREN'S RIGHTS |
| CHARITY |
| REFUGEES |
| ASYLUM SEEKERS |
| RICH AND POOR |
| AMBITION |
| ATTITUDES TO WEALTH |
| ANIMAL RIGHTS |
| VALUES |
| BLOOD SPORTS |
| VEGETARIANISM |

95

Help/Thinking skills

Commitment ladders

Commitment ladders can be used to show how committed you are to something. The higher up the ladder you go, the more committed you feel.

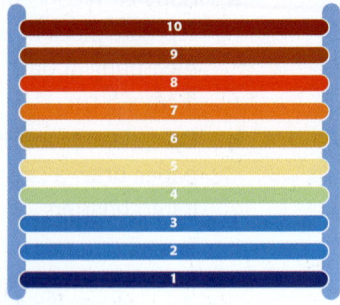

Concept maps

A concept map is a group of concepts linked to a topic or theme. You need to work out what you think the links and relationships are. Draw lines between the words and write on them what you think the links are.

Continuums

A continuum is a line along which you decide to place a word or idea and then discuss your decision with others.

Diamond nine activities

This is an activity where a list of things is rearranged in order of priority. The most important thing is placed at position 1. Continue to prioritise each item in the list until the least important is placed at position 9. You can do this on your own or in groups. In groups you will need to discuss your choices to reach a joint decision.

Fortune line graphs

Fortune lines help to explain feeling and emotions at different times. The horizontal axis is a timeline; the vertical axis represents emotions.

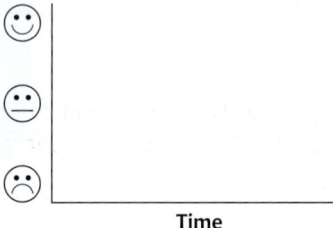

Freeze frame

This involves setting up a scene as if it were a video freeze frame or a still from a movie. You need to choose a scene from the story and freeze it. You need to be able to describe how each character in the freeze frame is thinking and feeling at that precise moment.

Light bulb test

Can you find an idea or a view to which you can give a light bulb? That means it lit up your thinking.

Living graphs

A living graph has two axes. One is a timeline and the other shows, for example, people's feelings. Often you will be given pieces of 'evidence' such as letters or statements, which are cut out and placed where you think they should go on a blank graph outline.

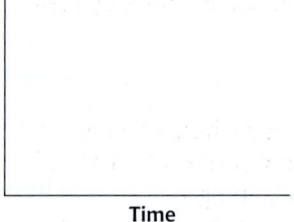

Map from memory

To produce a map from memory one member of each group comes to the front, looks at the image for ten seconds, returns to the group and draws what can be remembered. Each member of the group does the same and adds to the collective drawing that emerges from each group.

Help/Thinking skills

Mind maps

A mind map starts with a main idea or topic at the centre of a page with branches to sub topics which branch out further again. Use drawings and colours as well as writing the connections along the branches.

Sliding scales

This activity means using a scale of numbers from 1 to 5 to rank your response. 1 = Very hard to forgive and 5 = Very easy to forgive.

Spider diagrams

This is when a main idea (the body of the spider) is explored further (spider legs).

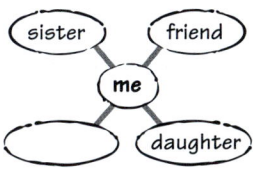

Stilling and meditation

Stilling is simply to be still and relaxed and meditation is to concentrate on something to help you think more deeply.

Storyboards

A storyboard is a visual way of telling a story. You can use a combination of flow charts, drawings, photos and text to show what happens, scene by scene.

Traffic lights

This is a technique where you rate each statement according to how you would respond.
Red = Definitely 'no go'
Amber = It's a possibility
Green = Go for it!

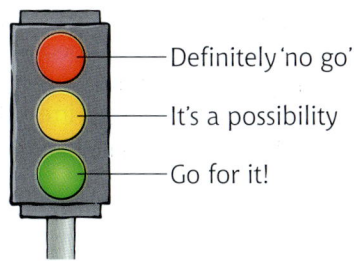

Venn diagrams

Venn diagrams show what things have in common, and what the differences are.

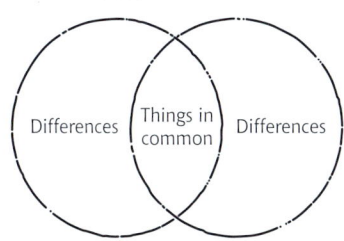

Zoom lens boards

A zoom lens board is five concentric circles on a large piece of paper. The central circle represents 'Most important', the second circle 'Very important', the third circle 'Important', the fourth circle 'Fairly important' and the fifth circle 'Least important'.

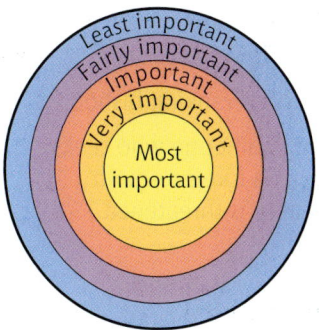

+ – ?

+ stands for what is good about it
– stands for what is bad about it
? stands for what you are not sure about it

5Ws

Discuss **what** it is, **where** and **when** you might see it, **who** might have it and **why**.

Key words

A

Adhan – the Muslim call to prayer, usually given from the minaret at a mosque

Advocacy – pleading or arguing a case for someone or something

Aggressor – someone who is responsible for the start of a conflict

Ahimsa – non-violence and respect for life

Amrit – a Sikh holy drink made of sugar and water that have been blessed. This term also refers to the ceremony of initiation into the Khalsa

Aqiqah – a Muslim ceremony seven days after birth when the baby's head is shaved to show that they are a servant of Allah. An animal is sacrificed in thanksgiving to Allah

Archbishop – a high-ranking bishop

Asylum seeker – someone who seeks help and safety in a foreign country because their safety is threatened where they live

Atonement – in Christianity, a restoring by Jesus of the relationship between God and mankind that had been broken by sin

Aum – the sacred symbol of Hinduism. It is also believed by Hindus to be the sound of the universe and is used as a mantra or prayer in itself

B

Baptise – to immerse in or sprinkle with water as a Christian symbolic act of joining the Church and being cleansed

Bar mitzvah – literally, 'son of the Commandment'. A Jewish boy's coming of age at 13 years old, marked by a ceremony in the synagogue and a family celebration

Bat mitzvah – literally, 'daughter of the Commandment'. A Jewish girl's coming of age at 12 years old

Bishop – a priest with responsibilities for a group of churches within a geographical area called a diocese

Breaking of bread – the sharing of bread and wine during a Christian service

Buddha – a title given to Siddhartha Gautama, the founder of Buddhism. It means the 'Enlightened One'

C

Captivity – a state of imprisonment or a situation where your freedom is taken away

Caste – a social system developed in ancient India in which people were divided into communities or castes. At the top were the Brahmins – priests, scholars and philosophers. The second highest caste were the Kshatriyas – the warriors and rulers. Third came the Vaishyas – traders, merchants and people involved in agricultural production. The lowest caste were the Shudras – labourers and servants for the other castes. Below even the Shudras were the untouchables. These people had no caste at all and performed the most menial jobs. Caste was determined by birth

Cathedral – the principal Christian church building of a bishop's diocese

Chaplain – a member of the clergy who conducts religious services and provides religious advice for those in places such as a prison, hospital or the armed forces

Charitable – refers to a person or organisation that is about generosity and care for those in some kind of need

Commitment – a strong belief in something shown by a promise to do something

Communist – someone committed to communism, a movement based on the ideas of Karl Marx and Lenin, and involving the abolition of classes and organised society

Community – a group of people who share the same interests or beliefs

Compassion – deep sympathy for the suffering of another person

Concentration camp – a camp where people were held and confined, usually under very harsh conditions

Confirmation – a ceremony to acknowledge a person's commitment to the Christian faith

Conflict – a state of prolonged disagreement, struggle, opposition, fighting or war

Conscience – the part of us that makes us aware of right and wrong actions

Curfew – a law or regulation requiring certain or all people to leave the streets or be at home at a certain time

D

Direct action – the use of different methods to achieve an objective, such as strikes and demonstrations

Discrimination – taking some kind of action against others based on your own prejudices

E

Empathy – being able to put oneself in someone else's shoes and understand their situation and feelings

Equality – where all people are treated the same and regarded as being equal in status, irrespective of wealth, importance, race or religion

Key words

Eucharist – sharing bread and wine during a Christian Anglican service

Evangelical – a Christian group or church that places particular emphasis on the Gospel and the scriptures as the sole authority in all matters of faith and behaviour

Evangelism – deriving from the Greek word meaning 'gospel', it refers to the zealous proclamation of Christianity by preachers and missionaries

F

Fairness – free of favouritism or bias and showing justice to all

Five Ks – the five symbols worn by Sikhs to express commitment to the Sikh faith. They are the kesh, kara, kanga, kaccha and kirpan. Guru Gobind Singh instructed Khalsa members to wear them

Forgiveness – willingness to show compassion and overlook wrong done against someone

Francis of Assisi – born in the twelfth century as the son of a rich cloth merchant, Francis gave up riches and founded the Franciscan order of monks devoted to preaching and living in poverty

Freedom – the right or the ability to do things without control or interference

Free will – the power to make choices for yourself

G

Golden Rule – found in some form in all religions, this can be summed up as 'treat others as you yourself would wish to be treated'

Gurdwara – a Sikh place of worship, also called a temple

Gurmukhi – literally, 'from the Guru's mouth'. The name given to the script in which the Sikh scriptures and the Punjabi language are written

Guru – literally, 'one who dispels darkness' or 'one who is heavy' with the weight of vast knowledge. A spiritual teacher and used of the ten Sikh spiritual leaders

Guru Gobind Singh – the tenth and last Guru. The founder of the Khalsa

Guru Granth Sahib – the Sikh holy book

Guru Nanak – the first Sikh spiritual leader or Guru and the founder of the Sikh faith

Haggadah – literally, 'to tell', it is the name given to the book that contains the order of service for the seder meal

Hajj – pilgrimage to Makkah in Saudi Arabia, which every Muslim is expected to perform at least once during their lifetime if they are physically and financially able

Harijan – literally, 'children of God', a term used by Gandhi to describe those who had previously been 'untouchable'

Harmony – agreement in opinion or action

Holocaust – from the Greek 'holos' (completely) and 'kaustos' (burned sacrificial offering), this refers to the Nazi extermination programme of Jews, gypsies, homosexuals and others who opposed Hitler's regime during the Second World War

Holy Communion – a service using bread and wine that recalls the last meal that Jesus shared with his disciples. It is also known as Eucharist or the Lord's Supper

Holy Liturgy – a service of worship with a prescribed ritual such as Evensong or Eucharist. Also a term used in the Orthodox Church for sharing bread and wine

Holy Spirit – the third person in the holy Trinity, with God the Father and God the Son

Holy war – a war fought on the basis of religion or religious differences

Hostage – a person held by one party in a conflict in order to make sure that a request will be met by the opposing party

Human rights – the basic rights and freedoms to which all people are entitled

I

Ihram – clothing worn by Muslims during Hajj (pilgrimage to Makkah). It consists of two pieces of plain, white, unsewn cloth and shows everyone is equal before Allah

Inequality – being treated unequally or not having the same opportunities

Injustice – something that is unfair and undeserved

IRA – a militant organisation of Irish nationalists who used terrorism to try to drive British forces from Northern Ireland and work for a united independent Ireland

Jihad – used by Muslims to mean striving for perfection. Also used to refer to a defensive war and used by some fundamentalist Muslims and others in the West to mean 'holy war'

Justice – what is morally right and fair

Just war – a term that originally came from a Christian explanation of what might be a morally acceptable war

Key words

K

Karma – a term used by Hindus, Sikhs and Buddhists to explain that all actions and thoughts affect a future rebirth

Khalsa – a Sikh term meaning 'community of the Pure'

Kippah – the skullcap worn by Jewish men, also called a yarmulke

L

Langar – literally, 'guru's kitchen', this refers to the dining hall in the gurdwara where everyone is welcome to eat free of charge

Lord's Supper – one of the terms used for sharing bread and wine during a Christian service

M

Makkah – Makkah is in Saudi Arabia and is the birthplace of the prophet Muhammad. The mosque in Makkah is the most important place of worship for Muslims around the world and a place of pilgrimage. All Muslims are required to face in the direction of the Ka'bah, a cube-shaped building in the centre of the mosque at Makkah, five times every day when offering their prayers

Mandir – a Hindu place of worship, also called a temple

Martyr – someone who makes a great sacrifice or even chooses to die because of a religious principle or belief

Mass – a service using bread and wine, practised by Roman Catholics

Mercy – willingness to be kind and forgiving towards someone who has done something wrong

Messiah – a Hebrew term meaning 'anointed one'. Jews believe he will bring in a new era for Judaism and all humankind. Christians believe he came in Jesus

Monastery – a community of monks who have committed themselves to a religious life that often means denying themselves comfort and luxury and living apart from the general community

Mosque – a Muslim place of worship

Muhammad – Muslims believe he is the last messenger of Allah

N

Nazi Party – a short term for National Socialist German Workers' Party, a right-wing, fascist and anti-semitic political party formed in 1919 and headed by Adolf Hitler from 1921 to 1945

Noble Eightfold Path – central to Buddhism, this describes how to live your life, how to end suffering and how to achieve Nirvana

Nun – a woman who belongs to a religious order and is devoted to active service or meditation, often living without everyday comforts

O

Oppression – the use of power in an excessive and cruel way

Orthodox – a traditional or historical belief. Used of the Christian Churches mainly in Eastern Europe and the Middle East, such as the Russian Orthodox Church and the Greek Orthodox Church

P

Pacifism – the belief that disputes between nations should be and can be settled peacefully and the unwillingness to use violence to settle a dispute

Pacifist – someone who believes war and violence are always wrong

Parable – a story often used by Jesus that involves a situation from everyday life and has a religious message

Paradise – used generally for a place of delight and beauty. In Christianity and Islam, it often refers to heaven. In Christianity it can be the place where souls await the resurrection of the dead

Pastor – literally, 'shepherd', the word for a Christian minister or priest who looks after a group of people or a church

Peace – this could refer to the absence of quarrels, disagreements and war or in a positive way to a state of harmony, quietness and tranquillity

Pentagon – the headquarters of the US military in Washington, USA

Persecution – causing others to suffer, especially those with different backgrounds or lifestyles, or those holding different religious beliefs

Pesach – the feast of Passover, celebrated by Jewish believers. The festival remembers how, when the Israelites were slaves in Egypt, the angel 'passed over' their homes after they had daubed their door posts with the blood of a lamb

Pharaoh – a term used to describe the ancient rulers of Egypt who were both political and religious leaders of the Egyptian people

Pilgrim – someone who makes a special journey to a religious place

Pilgrimage – a religious journey to a sacred place

Precept – a guideline or rule for Buddhist behaviour

Prejudice – to hold an opinion that is biased and unreasonable, and not based on real evidence

Prophet – a messenger of God

Key words

Punjab – a region in northern India that straddles the border between India and Pakistan. About 60 per cent of the population are Sikhs

Q

Qur'an – the Muslim holy book, revealed to the Prophet Muhammad by Allah through the Arch-Angel Gabriel over a period of 23 years, from 611 CE to 632 CE

R

Ramadan – the ninth month of the Muslim calendar and a time when Muslims fast from sunrise to sunset

Reconciliation – getting back into a relationship with someone. It could be with another person or, in a religious context, with God

Refugee – someone who leaves their country because of poverty, war, political reasons or persecution, and looks for help in another country

Reincarnation – a belief in the rebirth of the spirit or soul in a new body

Responsibilities – things you have a duty or obligation to do

Responsibility – the act of having a duty or obligation to do something

Resurrection – the central Christian belief that Jesus rose from the dead

Rites of passage – rituals or ceremonies marking events in someone's life when they move from one stage to another, such as getting married

Rosh Hashanah – a festival of the Jewish New Year, and a time when Jews recall the creation of the world

S

Sacrifice – giving up for a cause or faith something you value highly and would miss greatly

Salaam – means 'peace' and is an abbreviation of the Islamic greeting *as-salaamu 'alaykum* ('peace be upon you')

Samskara – Hindu sacraments designed to initiate a new stage of life. There are usually a total of 16 such rites of passage

Seder – literally, 'order', this refers to the meal eaten by Jews at Pesach

Segregation – the practice of separating people of different races, classes or ethnic groups in places such as schools, houses and other forms of public life as a form of discrimination

Shabbat – a Jewish day of rest from sunset on Friday to sunset on Saturday

Shofar – a ram's horn blown at the Jewish celebration of Rosh Hashanah

Socialist – someone who believes that the means of producing and distributing goods should be owned collectively by all

Stereotype – an over-simplified view or opinion that does not take into account all the facts and places someone or something too easily in a category

Symbol – something that represents something else

Synagogue – a place where Jewish people meet to worship and study

T

Tallit – a Jewish prayer shawl

Tefillin – small leather boxes containing passages from the Jewish Torah. These are strapped on the forehead and arm for morning prayers on weekdays

Torah – a Jewish holy book containing the first five books of the Old Testament

Torah – literally, 'teaching' or 'law', this refers to the first five books of the Hebrew scriptures: Genesis, Exodus, Leviticus, Numbers and Deuteronomy

Trade unionist – someone who is a member of an organisation (union) that aims to protect the interests of others in the same kind of job or trade

Turban – worn by Sikhs, the turban is a cloth covering the head. It is worn as a sign of devotion to God and obedience to the Sikh gurus

U

Ummah – the worldwide community of Muslims

Unfairness – an act that does not represent the truth, is biased and unjust

Unjust – unfair and contrary to what is morally or legally right

V

Volunteers – people who give help, perform a service or give their time to a cause freely

Y

Yad Vashem – Yad Vashem is the Holocaust memorial of the Jewish people. It is located on Har Hazikaron (the Mount of Remembrance) in Jerusalem, Israel and was established in 1953. It is a complex of museums, monuments, research, teaching and resource centres

Yom Kippur – a holy day for Jews

Z

Zakah – a tax on income to provide money for the poor and needy. The third pillar of Islam   .